FAITH
EVANGELISM™

Bobby H. Welch *and* **Doug Williams**

As Developed with **David Apple**

Revised by **G. Dwayne McCrary**

Foreword by **Thom Rainer**

LifeWay Press®
Nashville, Tennessee

ISBN 978-1-4158-6275-9
Item 005108884

This book is the resource for course CG-1314 in the subject areas Evangelism and Discipleship in the Christian Growth Study Plan.

Dewey decimal classification: 269.2
Subject headings: EVANGELISTIC WORK \ SUNDAY SCHOOLS

Unless indicated otherwise, Scripture quotations are taken from the Holman Christian Standard Bible®, copyright © 1999, 2000, 2002, 2003 by Holman Bible Publishers. Used by permission. Scripture quotations marked NIV are from the Holy Bible, New International Version, copyright © 1973, 1978, 1984 by International Bible Society.

FAITH Evangelism® is a registered trademark of LifeWay Christian Resources.

To order additional copies of this resource, write to LifeWay Church Resources Customer Service; One LifeWay Plaza; Nashville, TN 37234-0113; fax order to (615) 251-5933; e-mail *orderentry@lifeway.com*; phone toll free (800) 458-2772; order online at *www.lifeway.com*; or visit the LifeWay Christian Store serving you.

Printed in the United States of America

Leadership and Adult Publishing
LifeWay Church Resources
One LifeWay Plaza
Nashville, TN 37234-0175

CONTENTS

THE AUTHORS

BUILDING A STRONG FOUNDATION

Bobby Welch and Doug Williams, with David Apple, set a new direction for and focus on evangelism with the FAITH strategy and materials released in 1999.

BOBBY WELCH served America in the military, leaving the army with the rank of captain. As a platoon leader in Vietnam, he was shot and given up for dead, at which time God miraculously intervened in a life-changing way that resulted in Welch's call to the ministry.

Welch served as the pastor of First Baptist Church in Daytona Beach, Florida, from 1974 until he retired in August 2006. First Baptist originated the FAITH Sunday School Evangelism Strategy, merging evangelism with Sunday School.

Welch is the author of numerous books, including *Evangelism Through the Sunday School*, which introduced first-generation FAITH. He was also a major contributor to the original FAITH training materials.

Welch has served the Southern Baptist Convention in numerous leadership roles, including president (June 2004 to June 2006). In his first eight months as president, he spoke in all 50 states and Canada. The slogan "Everyone Can … and I'm It" quickly surfaced as a reminder that everyone has a role in and responsibility for personal evangelism. In March 2007 Welch was appointed the first strategist for global evangelical relations with the assignment of growing, maintaining, and nurturing Baptist cooperation on a global scale.

DOUG WILLIAMS has served as the national FAITH consultant for LifeWay Christian Resources since 1997 to the present and as the associate pastor/minister of education and evangelism at First Baptist Church in Daytona Beach, Florida, from 1982 to 1997. With Pastor Welch, Williams led First Baptist to combine Sunday School with evangelism training, an approach that became the forerunner of the first-generation FAITH strategy.

Williams teaches FAITH clinics throughout the United States and in other countries. His wife, Rachel, accompanies him to most clinics and is also active in FAITH. Together they have been involved in more than 65 consecutive 16-week semesters of evangelistic training. The couple resides in Oneonta, Alabama, where they are active in First Baptist Church and its FAITH ministry. They have three grown children.

DAVID APPLE is an adult ministry specialist for LifeWay Christian Resources, where he helps churches develop approaches for reaching the diversity of adults in their communities. A frequent writer, he is active in his Nashville church and especially enjoys assisting churches who are without a pastor during that transitional time. Apple worked with Bobby Welch and Doug Williams in developing the first-generation FAITH resources and strategy. He and his wife, Karen, have two grown children.

FAITH FOR THE FUTURE

Dwayne McCrary played a key role in responding to research about church practices in evangelism training and in revising and updating FAITH resources for a new generation of users.

G. DWAYNE MCCRARY is the minister of education at First Baptist Church in Nederland, Texas. Prior to that, he was the minister of young adults and discipleship at First Baptist Church in Lubbock, Texas, a FAITH originator church. An experienced writer for LifeWay Christian Resources, McCrary was on the team that developed Student FAITH Advanced and *FAITH Discipleship: Sharing a Living Faith.*

McCrary grew up in the home of a Baptist deacon and a church secretary. At the age of 16, he committed his life to Christ. He is married to Lisa, and they have two children, Bethany and Joshua. McCrary is currently working on his doctorate at New Orleans Baptist Theological Seminary.

Participating in the FAITH process has been a breath of fresh air for McCrary, with the Opinion Poll holding particular significance. Like many people, he had fears that grew from bad experiences in his past. The Opinion Poll helped McCrary overcome those fears and reintroduced him to the joy of visitation.

Pointing to 1 John 1:4, McCrary reminds us that we share Jesus to complete our joy, remembering the grace God has shown us. Dwayne, Lisa, and Bethany are trained in FAITH, and Dwayne looks forward to using these next-generation FAITH materials to train his son in the future.

FOREWORD

You are on this earth for two reasons: to glorify God and to make His name known among the nations. This is the mandate God gave to Abraham in Genesis 12:1-3 when He called Abraham out from the land of Haran. If you look closely at those verses, you'll see that God withholds no blessing from Abraham, but in the last half of verse 3 God tells him, "All the peoples of the earth will be blessed through you."

Think about it: how are all the peoples of the world blessed? Is it through material wealth, advancements in technology, or germ-free societies? All of these are blessings, but the most significant blessing anyone can receive, the only lasting blessing, is to be restored to a right relationship with the God of creation. If you look at a map of the world at the time of Abraham, the land God promised the Israelites sat exactly in the middle of all the trade routes of the day. As merchants passed through the land, God's plan was for His chosen people to proclaim His name among the nations.

God's plan has not changed. Jesus reiterated this call in His Great Commission (see Matt. 28:19-20). God's expectation was, and still is, that He be glorified and that we lead others to live as He intended—in a right relationship with Him through Jesus Christ.

That is the purpose of FAITH Evangelism. My desire is that through this resource you'll develop the skill of proclaiming God's name among the nations. No, I don't mean everyone should become missionaries in other cultures. Many should, and I pray that it happens; but God intends for us to start right where we are: with our next-door neighbors, family members, fellow students, coworkers—everywhere!

There is no greater time in history to share the message of saving faith through Christ. Research estimates that 160 million unchurched people live in America. Of those, 17 million will accept Christ if presented with the gospel. Even more compelling, another 43 million unchurched Americans are receptive to the gospel and to church. These numbers are staggering and exciting: 60 million unchurched people whom Jesus would classify as an abundant harvest (see Matt. 9:37).

Unfortunately, as Jesus lamented, the workers are few (see Matt. 9:37). Ironically, while people in America are more receptive to the gospel than ever before, research shows that Christians are becoming increasingly apathetic in their efforts to evangelize the lost. Jesus requested that we "pray to the Lord of the harvest to send out workers into His harvest" (Matt. 9:38).

EVANGELISM MATTERS

Your willingness to recognize the opportunity and step forward in commitment means that you are obeying Christ's command. You are among thousands who are pressing forward into the spiritual darkness to rescue precious lives from eternal separation with God. You are an answer to Jesus' prayer in Matthew 9:38.

My favorite verse of Scripture comes from Acts 4. Peter and John have just healed the man at the temple gates who had been crippled from birth. The people were amazed! The temple authorities were enraged. They dragged the disciples into court for an inquisition, then commanding them to stop preaching in the name of Jesus. Peter and John, with great boldness, responded, "Whether it's right in the sight of God for us to listen to you rather than to God, you decide; for we are unable to stop speaking about what we have seen and heard" (Acts 4:19-20).

That's my life verse, my passion. I never want to stop speaking about what I've seen and heard. Jesus has made too great a difference in my life for me to be silent. Think about the story: God wants to save sinners, but because of our sin and rebellion, we rightly deserve His punishment. For Him to be a just God, He has to punish us (see Prov. 17:15). How does God reconcile His desire to save sinners with His unwavering commitment to His standard of holiness? I'll let the Bible answer: "God, who is abundant in mercy, because of His great love that He had for us, made us alive with the Messiah even though we were dead in trespasses. By grace you are saved! He also raised us up with Him and seated us with Him in the heavens, in Christ Jesus" (Eph. 2:4-6). What a story! What great news! As the old hymn says,

> *Jesus paid it all.*
> *All to Him I owe.*
> *Sin had left a crimson stain.*
> *He washed it white as snow.*[1]

As you work through this invaluable training and move out into a hostile culture, go in confidence. The field is ready for harvest. God wants to save sinners. Jesus paid it all. I commission you with the words of Paul: "How, then, can they call on the one they have not believed in? And how can they believe in the one of whom they have not heard? And how can they hear without someone preaching to them? And how can they preach unless they are sent? As it is written, 'How beautiful are the feet of those who bring good news!' " (Rom. 10:14-15, NIV).

I pray that the desperately lost will see your feet as beautiful as you glorify God by making His name known among the nations.

A GREAT PASTOR LEADS OUT

Never underestimate the influence of a great pastor. That statement summarizes a study LifeWay Research completed in January 2007 on what separates evangelistic churches from those that are not reaching their communities for Christ. Much talk in the Southern Baptist Convention (SBC) centers on evangelism and our effectiveness in following Jesus' command to reach people with the gospel. Our denomination and other denominations are seeing declining church memberships and a general ineffectiveness in reaching people for Christ. Basically, we have been charged with a job, and we are not getting the job done.

But as this research revealed, there are bright spots. Twenty-two churches in the SBC met specified criteria for what constitutes evangelistically effective churches. Nineteen of those churches agreed to participate in a one-to-one interview survey to explore reasons they are effective. Research teams found that the most common element in these churches is how strongly the senior pastor sets the tone for an emphasis on evangelism. He makes it a passion and a priority.

What is equally evident is the humility with which these men lead their churches to reach lost souls. Humility is the point at which we must all begin if we are to exponentially improve our effectiveness in seeing people come to Christ.

It is easy to become isolated and to see our churches as a refuge where we get away from the increasing rawness of our culture. Church was never meant to be a retreat center but a triage center and a critical-care unit for the spiritually ill. A great pastor with a passion for practicing emergency care can guide church members to look outward. Not only does he turn their eyes to the fields, he also leads them into the harvest. Never underestimate a great pastor's influence to infuse the congregation with a passion for the lost.[2]

THOM RAINER
President and CEO, LifeWay Christian Resources

1. Elvina M. Hall, "Jesus Paid It All," *The Baptist Hymnal* (Nashville: Convention Press, 1991), 134.
2. Adapted from Thom Rainer, "The Passionate Pastor," *Facts & Trends,* May–June 2007.

ENGAGING A NEEDY WORLD IN FAITH

In an ever-changing, increasingly complex world, the gospel of Jesus Christ remains the same. People's need for salvation does not and will not change. FAITH Evangelism is all about Christians and churches engaging their part of the world with the message and the Savior people so desperately need—and doing so with courage, sensitivity, and intentionality.

For this reason FAITH Evangelism training begins and ends with the gospel—with Christ's Great Commission—inviting believers to experience the joy of knowing Him in a more personal way as they commit to share His good news with others. The 12 sessions in this resource are your starting point for expressing this commitment.

By prayerfully accepting the important role of FAITH team learner, you are demonstrating your compassion for the lost and a heart for evangelism. These qualities will be important as you participate in these sessions and actively share your faith with others.

Dependence on the Holy Spirit is never more necessary than when Christians actively share their faith. FAITH teams can expect spiritual warfare as they begin training and start reaching out to their circle of friends and acquaintances.

As you bathe FAITH Evangelism in prayer, you can anticipate that God will work in significant ways in your life. You can expect to change and develop in the following ways.

- You will grow as a devoted follower of Christ.
- You will begin to model evangelism as a lifestyle and as a way of thinking. As you study, practice, and watch your team leader carry out evangelism and ministry, you will be better able to carry out evangelism and ministry yourself.
- You will gain competence in initiating spiritual dialogue and moving into a presentation of the gospel as you experience a variety of visitation settings.
- You will develop as a leader, increasingly willing and able to take on more responsibility within the body of Christ.

If your church does its primary outreach through Sunday School, you will find that FAITH training can strengthen and streamline the ministry of these open Bible study groups. If your church does ministry primarily through small groups, you will find that FAITH is flexible, allowing for training to be done in a small-group setting—or even by one team leader personally mentoring two learners through this training process. No matter how your church chooses to do FAITH training, this resource follows this weekly schedule:

- *Team Time*—15 minutes of learning the gospel presentation and discussing home-study assignments
- *Teaching Time*—45 minutes of classroom training
- *Visitation Time*—approximately 1½ hours of intentional visits by teams
- *Celebration Time*—30 minutes of celebration when teams return from visits

The following statement by one FAITH learner named Kathy sums up the goals and possibilities of FAITH training.

> *FAITH training has given me the confidence to share Christ with anyone at any time. The training enabled me to be prepared at a moment's notice. I would never have been that bold, even though I wanted to be. The Lord has demonstrated time and time again that if I'm prepared and willing to obey, He will go before me.*

TOOLS FOR YOUR JOURNEY

Congratulations! You have set God-sized goals—to give evangelism priority in your church, to become equipped to penetrate your community with the gospel, to become an authentic minister on a day-by-day basis, and to grow in personal faith in Christ.

Your **FAITH journal** will help you achieve these goals as you place yourself under the Holy Spirit's direction and your church's leadership. By reading your journal, participating in group sessions, and practicing the FAITH **gospel presentation** (see pp. 10–11), you will learn how to share Christ and to adapt and use the FAITH outline in different situations. Conversation starters are suggested throughout the semester to help you personalize FAITH.

Your journal will also lead you to take your FAITH journey deeper each week through five home-study assignments called **"My FAITH Journey."** To be completed the week following your group session, "My FAITH Journey" will take you deeper into the concepts you have studied, will give you new ideas for reaching out to the lost persons in your life, and will prepare you for your next group session.

Another important component of your journal, called **"My FAITH Connections,"** will help you stay on track with your personal goals for spiritual growth and witnessing during the week between group sessions. This weekly checklist provides space to record visitation and life-witness opportunities you may have, important developments in your walk with the Lord, progress in your FAITH assignments, and a prayer list for the lost persons you know.

In your weekly group sessions your facilitator may use a variety of tools to help you learn the FAITH gospel presentation and to effectively reach your lost friends, acquaintances, and family members. For example, the **facilitator guide enhanced CD** provides additional content for selected sessions, supplemental articles on reaching the lost, FAITH forms and tools, and a PowerPoint presentation to use in group sessions.

An **audio version** of the FAITH outline is also included on your facilitator's CD. The facilitator has permission to burn this file to CDs for you and your team members. Also, three **songs** written especially for FAITH can motivate, add variety, and help you and other participants learn.

Video segments are available on DVD to support most sessions. Your facilitator has options for when and how to use video. He or she can choose the DVD dramatic vignettes or show parts of the presentation to teach F-A-I-T-H (including the Invitation). The dramatic vignettes follow two FAITH teams in continuing story lines as lives and FAITH experiences intersect.

Two leaflets represent an important part of every team's visitation folder— **A Step of Faith** and **Next Steps in Following Jesus**. Teams will use these in visits to share the gospel and follow up on new believers. This course provides training on how to use these tools in visits.

Prayer Partner Commitment Card helps ground FAITH in prayer, and **FAITH Outline Card** can be kept in a purse or pocket to use as witnessing opportunities arise.

FAITH GOSPEL PRESENTATION

In your personal opinion, what do you understand it takes for a person to get to heaven and have eternal life?

F IS FOR *FORGIVENESS*

Everyone has sinned and needs God's forgiveness.
"All have sinned and fall short of the glory of God."
Romans 3:23

God's forgiveness is in Jesus only.
"In Him we have redemption through His blood, the forgiveness of our trespasses, according to the riches of His grace."
Ephesians 1:7

A IS FOR *AVAILABLE*

God's forgiveness is available for all.
"God loved the world in this way: He gave His One and Only Son, so that everyone who believes in Him will not perish but have eternal life."
John 3:16

God's forgiveness is available but not automatic.
"Not everyone who says to Me, 'Lord, Lord!' will enter the kingdom of heaven."
Matthew 7:21

I IS FOR *IMPOSSIBLE*

According to the Bible, it is impossible to get to heaven on our own.
"By grace you are saved through faith, and this is not from yourselves; it is God's gift—not from works, so that no one can boast."
Ephesians 2:8-9

So how can a sinful person have eternal life and enter heaven?

T IS FOR *TURN*

If you were going down the road and someone asked you to turn, what would he or she be asking you to do? *(Change direction)*

Turn means *repent*.

Turn away from sin and self.

"Unless you repent, you will all perish as well!"
Luke 13:3

Turn to Jesus alone as your Savior and Lord.

"I am the way, the truth, and the life. No one comes to the Father except through
  Me."
John 14:6

Here is the greatest news of all.

"If you confess with your mouth, 'Jesus is Lord,' and believe in your heart that
  God raised Him from the dead, you will be saved. With the heart one believes,
  resulting in righteousness, and with the mouth one confesses, resulting in
  salvation."
Romans 10:9-10

What happens if a person is willing to repent of their sins and confess Christ?

H IS FOR *HEAVEN*

Heaven is a place where we will live with God forever.

"If I go away and prepare a place for you, I will come back and receive you
  to Myself, so that where I am you may be also."
John 14:3

Eternal life begins now with Jesus.

"I have come that they may have life and have it in abundance."
John 10:10

H can also stand for *how.*

How can a person have God's forgiveness, eternal life, and heaven?
By trusting Jesus as your Savior and Lord.

INVITATION

Inquire

Understanding what we have shared, would you like to receive this forgiveness
by trusting in Christ as your personal Savior and Lord?

Invite

Insure

EXPRESSION OF COMMITMENT

I commit myself to FAITH Evangelism training in my church.

I recognize FAITH training as a way to help my church,

to grow as a Great Commission Christian, and to obey

God's command to be an active witness.

Signed _____

I will faithfully attend and participate in this semester of FAITH training

as a   ☐ team leader   ☐ team learner

My team members _____

My Sunday School department, class, or small group _____

Dates of my FAITH Evangelism training _____

SESSION

THE GREAT ADVENTURE

SESSION GOALS

You will—
- discover what it means to be a disciple maker;
- realize the need our world has for Christ;
- identify key elements of the Great Commission Christ gave us;
- describe goals and benefits of FAITH training;
- outline a process for enlisting prayer partners;
- look with expectancy toward the changes God will bring through obedience to Him.

Have you ever wondered what it might have been like to be one of the sailors on the Nina, Pinta, and Santa Maria as they left the port with Columbus in 1492? Their purpose was simple: to prove they could gain access to Asia by sea and thus open a new route for trading with Asia. No priests, soldiers, or settlers were on any of the ships; all were either sailors or government officials ready to explore and discover. The sailors were simply to go, get proof that they had been to the new land, return, and tell everyone about their discoveries. Theirs was the ultimate adventure.

When you think about adventure, what comes to your mind? _____

_____

_____

_____

God is inviting you to go on a _____ _____ with Him. This invitation includes:

- Being a _____ _____: "All authority has been given to Me in heaven and on earth. Go, therefore, and make disciples of all nations, baptizing them in the name of the Father and of the Son and of the Holy Spirit, teaching them to observe everything I have commanded you. And remember, I am with you always, to the end of the age" (Matt. 28:18-20).
- Being a _____ of _____: " 'Follow Me,' He told them, 'and I will make you fish for people!' " (Matt. 4:19).
- Being _____ and _____: "You are the salt of the earth. But if the salt should lose its taste, how can it be made salty? It's no longer good for anything but to be thrown out and trampled on by men. You are the light of the world. A city situated on a hill cannot be hidden" (Matt. 5:13-14).
- Being an _____: "We are ambassadors for Christ; certain that God is appealing through us, we plead on Christ's behalf, 'Be reconciled to God' " (2 Cor. 5:20).

These roles involve more than attending church and tithing. Discipleship is about developing a lifelong—really an eternal—_____ with God (see Rev. 3:20). He wants to reveal Himself to us, letting us know His heart, His character, and His love for us.

Some of your answers in the previous activity most likely describe the adventure God wants us to have with Him. In what ways could the words you used to describe adventure also characterize the relationship God wants to have with you?

_____

_____

_____

_____

_____

As we come to know God more intimately, we learn that His desire is for us to
_____ _____ what we have found. Being salt, light, and ambassadors all
include the idea of sharing with others. John declared it this way:

> What was from the beginning,
> what we have heard,
> what we have seen with our eyes,
> what we have observed,
> and have touched with our hands,
> concerning the Word of life—
> that life was revealed,
> and we have seen it
> and we testify and declare to you
> the eternal life that was with the Father
> and was revealed to us—
> what we have seen and heard
> we also declare to you,
> so that you may have fellowship along with us;
> and indeed our fellowship is with the Father
> and with His Son Jesus Christ.
> 1 John 1:1-3

John reminded his readers that he was simply telling what he had seen and
experienced for himself.

In the same way, John reminds us that we don't have to know all the hows and
whats to share Jesus with others. We are not responsible for explaining what
we haven't discovered yet. All we are asked to do is tell what we know and have
personally discovered.

The story is told of a college professor who taught philosophy. The final exam was
a one-question test—a question that had not been discussed or covered in class
or in the textbook. The professor had done this to observe his students' reactions.
Most students got up and walked out, not knowing how to respond. One student
read the question and began to write feverishly. He wrote until no time was left.

The professor picked up the paper and began to read: "I don't know, nor have I
ever considered the issues related to this question. It would be a practice in futility
for me to respond to something I have not truly studied or analyzed. However, there
are some things I do know." From that point on, the student presented a summary
of his class notes and the insights he had gained through the class experiences.
The professor looked at the student, commended him, wrote an A across the top
of the paper, and left the room.

In his Gospel John introduced us to a man born blind (see John 9). Jesus' healing
caused a stir in the city. Everyone was filled with questions, even the religious
leaders. All kinds of accusations were made. The religious leaders even declared
Jesus to be a sinner because He had performed this miracle on the Sabbath. When
confronted by these religious leaders, the man who had been healed responded
by saying, "Whether or not He's a sinner, I don't know. One thing I do know: I was
blind, and now I can see!" (John 9:25). Likewise, we can find comfort in realizing
that we are to tell what we _____ and what we have _____. That is what
being a _____ is all about.

THE NEED

The sailors with Columbus were trying to address a crisis their country faced. The Ottoman Empire, which had already conquered much of southeastern Europe, had captured the city of Constantinople in 1453, closing an important trade route from Europe to the east. European merchants could still buy Asian goods, but now they had to go through a new middleman. They were unable to purchase the products directly. Their economic future depended on finding a new way to trade directly with Asian merchants.

Think about the various crises our world faces today. List some news stories from the past week that point to needs our world faces today.

_____

_____

_____

_____

_____

As you look at your list, circle the issues arising from spiritual needs.

The ultimate need of our world is a relationship with its Creator. The majority of people in our world have no idea about their need for God or how to deal with the _____ that separates them from God. Jesus _____ to the need by leaving the glory of heaven, taking on the form of a human, and sacrificing Himself in the cruelest of ways so that we could have forgiveness of our sin. During FAITH training we will examine why Jesus had to sacrifice Himself for us, gaining a better understanding of our need for salvation. Jesus understood the need.

In our world today people live and die without _____. In the United States alone 2.5 million people die annually. It is estimated that _____ percent of the current U.S. population is lost without Christ.[1] If you do the math, that means every hour in the United States, _____ people die without Christ.[2] This doesn't even address the need in other countries. We must respond to humanity's need for Christ, following His example.

How would you describe our world's need for Christ? _____

_____

_____

_____

_____

_____

_____

What kind of difference do you think it would make if more people were followers of Jesus?

_____

_____

_____

_____

THE GOOD NEWS

The exciting news is that people are seeking to discover the _____ about _____ _____. Research done by Thom Rainer and his staff revealed that 82 percent of the unchurched were somewhat likely to attend church if invited. If only half of that 82 percent actually came, that would represent 80 million people in the United States alone![3] This same research showed that the overwhelming majority of the unchurched would like to develop a sincere relationship with a Christian. Their concern for their children is one factor driving this desire, but so is the desire to dialogue about spiritual matters.

The unchurched are not as concerned about being preached to as they are about being invited to go along on our journey of faith. They want to know what we are discovering, how God makes a difference in our lives, and how they can discover Him as well.

Jesus gave us the charge to _____ with the unchurched as He was about to return to heaven after His crucifixion. He told His followers, "All authority has been given to Me in heaven and on earth. Go, therefore, and make disciples of all nations, baptizing them in the name of the Father and of the Son and of the Holy Spirit, teaching them to observe everything I have commanded you. And remember, I am with you always, to the end of the age" (Matt. 28:18-20). Jesus' words, which we know as the _____ _____, serve as our marching orders as Christians.

The Great Commission tells us what we are to do with what we have seen. _____ _____—_____, _____, and _____— is the backbone of our mission as a church and as individual believers. *Baptize* and *teach* define what it means to be salt, light, and an ambassador for Christ.

When you became a Christian, you were baptized as a public declaration of your faith in Jesus. Other believers came alongside you and taught you how to live the Christian life and build a relationship with God. In a way, being a part of FAITH training is another part of your discipleship training. The assignment Jesus gave was for each of us to seek to share _____ with others; to see them make a _____ to Him; and then to _____ _____ them, showing them the ropes of the Christian life.

These descriptions of our task are sandwiched between two important promises:
1. We will have His _____. Jesus began the Great Commission by declaring His power and rule (see Matt. 28:18). Power and authority were given to Him as a result of His death on the cross, for through His death He paid the penalty for sin and thus defeated the power of sin and death (see Eph. 1:7). In His commission Jesus reminded us that He has the power to defend us when we go. He will help us face tests and dangers. Even if going costs us our lives, He has the power to give us eternal life (see Luke 9:24). All Columbus and his sailors had was a

proclamation from the Spanish monarchy. The One who has the power to overcome death and give life offers us His full power when we go in His name.

2. We will have His _____ (see Matt. 28:20). Jesus promised not only to give us His power but also to be with us as we go. Paul reminded Timothy, "God has not given us a spirit of fearfulness, but one of power, love, and sound judgment" (2 Tim. 1:7). During the week leading to His crucifixion, Jesus was honest with His followers about what was about to happen. They understood that He was about to die and would not be with them anymore (see John 16:28). They had given Him three years of their lives and had left everything to follow Him. You can imagine the fears and anxiety these followers must have felt as they wrestled with this reality. However, Jesus promised that He would not leave them alone, but another One just like Him would come (see John 14:15-18). This other One is the _____ _____. He does many things, including live within each believer. The followers of Jesus would never need to worry about being alone again.

POWER OVER OUR FEARS

A number of things can keep us from sharing with another person about Jesus. List some of those things.

_____

_____

_____

_____

_____

_____

Review your list and circle all the reasons that relate to fear.

If we are honest, we must admit that we have some fears about witnessing. Sometimes we may get a little nervous about sharing with another person. We may be nervous about answering questions, fumbling over our words, or forgetting a Bible passage. Or maybe we are afraid of the response we might receive. We cannot let these fears dominate our lives. One purpose of FAITH is to help you know what _____ to share and to gain _____ in God so that you can overcome your fears about witnessing.

Some fear is good because it reminds us of the _____ of what we are about to do and forces us to _____ on _____. We are not capable of changing this world; only Jesus can do that. Our responsibility is to introduce others to Him and to let them decide for themselves what they will do with Jesus.

The Holy Spirit will use you to help bring about conviction of a person's need for Jesus (see John 16:8). Apart from Him we are powerless. As you go out on visits and as you cultivate relationships each day, you will discover people who have been asking God to send someone to them for spiritual help. If we make ourselves available, He will _____ us in ways we never could have imagined.

FAITH training includes both going out as part of a team of three persons and taking every opportunity to share Jesus with others in our daily lives. Each team has a team leader who has completed at least one semester of FAITH training; he or she will _____ you. You will go out each week to represent _____, your_____, and your _____ _____ _____ or _____ _____. Although not everyone you visit or meet would attend your Sunday School class, he or she would likely be open to attending another class or small group in your church. As a result, you serve as a _____ between your Sunday School and your community. That link also supports you as you go.

The ultimate goal of FAITH is to help Christians become _____ _____, equipped to introduce others to Christ and then help them begin to mature as Christians and ultimately become disciple makers themselves.

What goals do you have for sharing Jesus? Describe what you hope to accomplish by being involved in FAITH training.

_____

_____

_____

_____

_____

THE SOURCE OF POWER

One element essential to success in witnessing is _____. God's promised power and presence are functions of prayer. When we go to share with others about Jesus, we place ourselves on the frontlines of spiritual battle.

In Exodus 17 we learn that Moses stood with his hands raised on top of the hill overlooking the battle between Israel and the Amalekites. As long as Moses' hands were raised, Israel prevailed. When Moses' arms became weary and his hands came down, the Amalekites would prevail. So Moses sat on a stone, and Aaron and Hur stood on each side of him and held up his arms. Israel prevailed, and the Amalekites were defeated.

We need partners who will be our Aaron and Hur as we go into battle. These persons are our _____ _____. Here is what we need to do to help and receive help from our prayer partners.

1. Recruit at least _____ prayer partners. Potential prayer partners are all around you:
   • *Your Sunday School class or other small group.* Try to enlist at least one prayer partner from your class or Bible study group.
   • *Your home.* One prayer partner could be a family member.
   • *Church friends.* You may know someone you would like to enlist who is a member of your church but is not a family member or a member of your Sunday School class or small group.
   • *New believers.* If you know friends who recently accepted Christ, invite them to pray with you. Being lost is fresh on their minds, and that memory can add urgency to their prayers.

2. Using the Prayer Partner Commitment Card, share _____ with your prayer partners. Explain that each week you will count on them to pray for you as you go out and as you are salt and light during the week. Help them understand that the purpose of this partnership is to band together to win your community for Christ. You may want to ask them to hold you _____ for sharing with people daily.

3. Set aside a _____ _____ to pray with your prayer partners, perhaps for approximately 15 minutes each week. The focus of this time must be your FAITH ministry. You can meet with them separately or together, perhaps in conjunction with a regularly scheduled church activity.

4. Ask them to _____ to pray for you, using the FAITH Prayer Partner Commitment Card. Record all contact information for each prayer partner, as well as the time and place you will meet. Ask each partner to sign the card. Give each one a copy of the card to keep. Highlight the prayer suggestions on the back of the card.

5. Ask if you can _____ your prayer partners before leaving the church for visits. Your prayer partners can pray _____ _____ for the person(s) your team is scheduled to visit. This gives your partner more of a personal connection and excitement when decisions are made public.

6. Look for opportunities to _____ prayer partners in ways other than prayer. The most asked question at the end of a FAITH training session has to be "Where will I get my learners for the next semester?" The best place to locate future learners is the prayer-partner pool. These individuals have spent weeks praying for FAITH participants, praying for lost persons, and listening to accounts of answered prayer. Many of these prayer partners will ask you whether they can be learners next semester. Others will not think to ask but will be willing if you approach them.

As you meet to share and pray with your partners, you will get to know these Christian brothers and sisters as you have never known them before. You will build _____ that will continue after FAITH training is complete. You will be _____ to know that these prayer partners are supporting all of your training and witnessing efforts through prayer.[4]

JOIN THE CREW

The irony of Christopher Columbus's adventure was that finding a crew was almost impossible. Because it was supported by the monarchy, the voyage received a great deal of attention. You would think this support and the thrill of adventure would be more than enough to entice sailors to go. But in reality willing sailors were so greatly needed that freedom was offered to criminals if they would sign up for the journey! Those who declined turned down the opportunity to make a significant difference in history. Proving that they could reach Asia by sea would begin an economic revolution. Everything would change, even geography and science textbooks.

Take a look at the graph on the following page, paying close attention to the last two items.

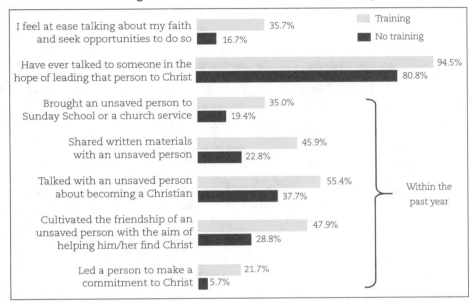

Southern Baptists who have received training in sharing their faith versus those without training

	Training	No training	Within the past year
I feel at ease talking about my faith and seek opportunities to do so	35.7%	16.7%	
Have ever talked to someone in the hope of leading that person to Christ	94.5%	80.8%	
Brought an unsaved person to Sunday School or a church service	35.0%	19.4%	
Shared written materials with an unsaved person	45.9%	22.8%	
Talked with an unsaved person about becoming a Christian	55.4%	37.7%	
Cultivated the friendship of an unsaved person with the aim of helping him/her find Christ	47.9%	28.8%	
Led a person to make a commitment to Christ	21.7%	5.7%	

Notice that there is a _____ _____ between the lives of those who have been trained to share their faith and those who have not. Research indicates a _____ percent possibility that you will develop a friendship this year with an unchurched person and engage him or her in an ongoing dialogue about spiritual things, including salvation.[5]

Greater than that, think about others in your church who are being trained or have been trained to share their faith in Jesus. Try to identify four such persons. You make the fifth person in that group. There is a high probability that one of the five of you will lead at least one person to Christ this year.

Only one hundred sailors were willing to sail with Columbus on that journey long ago. Because they were willing to go on the adventure, however, they had a part in changing the world as they knew it. Through your involvement in FAITH, you too have the same opportunity, but the difference you make will have _____ significance:

1. You will impact _____ by helping others find the way. Because of you, people will spend eternity with Jesus.
2. You will impact your _____. This world needs help. The only lasting solutions are found in a relationship with God. As you help others discover the truth of the gospel, you make your world a better place.
3. You will make a difference in your _____. New excitement will be created as people accept Christ. New Sunday School classes will be needed. Wouldn't it be exciting if every worship service included baptism?

At least one more person will be changed as a result of FAITH training: that person is _____. Kathy discovered firsthand the difference FAITH can make. Read her testimony.

FAITH training has truly changed my life. First, it has given me the confidence to share Christ with anyone at any time. The training enabled me to be prepared at a moment's notice. I would never have been that bold, even though I wanted to be. The Lord has demonstrated time and time again that if I'm prepared and willing to obey, He will go before me. The results are between the Holy Spirit and the lost. God is faithful. When I obey, He gives me perfect peace.

The result of this perfect peace has strengthened my relationship with the Lord. God continues to stretch my faith, producing more growth and maturity in my life. In addition to my spiritual growth, God has given me new friends. Many of my closest relationships with other believers were formed as a result of being on the same FAITH team. These friends continue to be a source of love and encouragement. We have been through some spiritual battles together, and we have seen God use us as a team to make a difference. I know I have friends I can trust no matter what.

As you begin your adventure of FAITH, you are making a commitment to represent God to this world. You will be challenged to do new things, stretching your faith. You will see God use you to make a difference in someone's life. You will gain new friends you know you can trust. Enjoy the adventure and the new discoveries you will make about yourself, God, and His redemptive purpose for all the world.

1. LifeWay research report, 10 March 2006.
2. Ibid.
3. Thom Rainer, *The Unchurched Next Door: Understanding Faith Stages as Keys to Sharing Your Faith* (Grand Rapids, MI: Zondervan, 2003), 24–25.
4. Adapted from Lawrence H. Phipps, *Praying in Faith Facilitator Guide* (Nashville: LifeWay Press, 2002), 38–41. Out of print.
5. "U. S. Congregational Life Survey: Conversion and Witnessing Among Southern Baptists," *Research Report* (Alpharetta, GA: Research Services, North American Mission Board, SBC, Summer 2002).

MY FAITH CONNECTIONS

Visitation Summary

Attempts   _____

Completed visits   _____

Key Question asked   _____

Record a synopsis of your team's visits. Include actions you may need to take on needs discovered. Whom should you tell about these needs? Prayer partners? Sunday School teacher? Minister?

_____

_____

_____

_____

Life-Witness Summary

Key Question asked   _____

_____

_____

_____

_____

_____

My Journey This Week

What has God taught you this week? Record insights you have gained about God and yourself.

_____

_____

_____

_____

To-Do List

☐ Read session 1
☐ Completed "My FAITH Journey":
   ☐ Day 1
   ☐ Day 2
   ☐ Day 3
   ☐ Day 4
   ☐ Day 5

☐ Completed evangelistic story
☐ Contacted prayer partners
☐ Began memorizing FAITH outline
☐ _____
☐ _____
☐ _____
☐ _____
☐ _____
☐ _____

Prayer List

Lost people for whom you are praying:
☐ _____
☐ _____
☐ _____
☐ _____
☐ _____
☐ _____
☐ _____
☐ _____
☐ _____
☐ _____
☐ _____
☐ _____

Others needing prayer:
☐ _____
☐ _____
☐ _____
☐ _____
☐ _____
☐ _____
☐ _____
☐ _____
☐ _____
☐ _____
☐ _____

DAY 1

The stage was set, and everything was ready. For the first time in history, the king of England would make a radio address that would be heard not only by the people of England but also by the world. The radio broadcast would be sent by wire across the Atlantic Ocean to be heard live on CBS radio in the United States. Just as King George was about to give the opening address at the London Arms Conference, the unthinkable happened. One of the control-room staffers tripped over the wire and broke it. Seeing that the connection had been severed, Harold Vidian sprang into action, grabbing the two ends of the broken wire. Two hundred and fifty volts of electricity went through his arms, but he was able to hang on. Because of Harold, people in the United States tuned in to CBS radio that day and heard the king's message.[1]

When you read this story, what thoughts come to your mind? _____

_____

_____

What do you think others thought when Harold took this action? _____

_____

What do you think Harold thought? _____

_____

How is Harold's action similar to being a witness for Jesus? _____

_____

_____

_____

Harold knew that what he was about to do would be an adventure. It is not every day that you intentionally grab hold of 250 volts of electricity! He also knew that if he didn't act, people in the United States would not receive the message. Harold was the only fix available that would make possible the delivery of the message.

Similarly, the line between God and the world has been severed. God is looking for some Harold Vidians to grab hold of the severed line and make it possible for His message to be heard. That is God's invitation to be a disciple maker. The Bible tells us, "God has not given us a spirit of fearfulness, but one of power, love, and sound judgment" (2 Tim. 1:7).

That severed line between God and the world is sitting in front of you right now. By being a part of FAITH training, you are taking steps toward the severed wire. Ask God to help you take hold and be a conduit of His power so that His message can be heard.

1. John Jess, "The Chapel of the Air," radio message 1123.

DAY 2

Review "Power over Our Fears," beginning on page 18. The Holy Spirit is actively involved in helping us share the gospel. Through His power that lives in us, we are able to go and share with others. No coach would send a team out to play a game without first preparing the players. Regardless of how much the coach teaches, ultimately, some things are up to the players. They have to listen to what the coach tells them and do their part.

When we go visit or otherwise engage ourselves in people's lives, we have to do our part. We have to prepare ourselves to become authentic fishers of men in today's world.

How do you need to prepare yourself to be used by the Holy Spirit? _____

_____

What are you doing to place yourself in a position to hear from God? _____

_____

When Jesus promised the Holy Spirit, He told the disciples what the Holy Spirit would do for them. Read John 14:15-18,25-26; 16:5-15 and list the things Jesus promised the Holy Spirit would do.

_____

_____

_____

Put a check beside the action that excites you most. Why did you select that action?

_____

_____

_____

Circle the actions that will help you be a witness. Explain how these actions of the Holy Spirit will help you witness.

_____

_____

_____

_____

Thank God for providing the Holy Spirit in your life and ask that He help you witness to one person in the next 24 hours.

DAY 3

Describe your life before you were a Christian. _____

_____

_____

_____

_____

_____

_____

Describe your life after you became a Christian. _____

_____

_____

_____

_____

_____

_____

We all have a story to tell. Most of us are more than ready to tell others about our lives. The most important part of our story is the difference Jesus makes in our lives. In the previous session we discovered a man whose sight Jesus restored (see John 9). He had a story to tell. The woman at the well met Jesus and then told her city about the encounter (see John 4). She had a story to tell. Paul was traveling to Damascus to persecute Christians when Jesus appeared (see Acts 22). He too had a story to tell.

Sharing our evangelistic story is a natural tool we have for initiating dialogue about spiritual things. On pages 34–35 you will find more information about your evangelistic story.

Using the headings found on pages 34–35, write your evangelistic story on a separate sheet of paper. Use the guidelines on pages 34–35 to assist you. Make sure you can share your story in three minutes or less.

You may want to ask one of your prayer partners to evaluate and respond to what you have written. Bring a copy of your evangelistic story with you to the next session.

MY FAITH JOURNEY

DAY 4

Have you ever wished you could wear just one hat at a time? Wouldn't it be more enjoyable sometimes to be at a ball game at which a relative was playing and you could set your dad, mom, or sibling hat to the side and put on your fan hat? We can't do that because no matter what, we are still dad, mom, or sibling. We occupy that role 24 hours a day.

Some may think FAITH training is the preparation-for-organized-visitation hat. The fact is, although FAITH helps with organized visitation, the real goal of FAITH training is for each of us to become more like Christ as we relate to others in every part of our lives. FAITH is not something you do for three hours a week and then stop doing the rest of the week.

We learned in session 1 that going on a great adventure with God includes being an ambassador for Him. When writing to the Corinthian church, Paul stated, "We are ambassadors for Christ; certain that God is appealing through us, we plead on Christ's behalf, 'Be reconciled to God' " (2 Cor. 5:20). Ambassadors represent their country all the time. Even when in another country, ambassadors are never excused from that duty.

The same is true of ambassadors for Christ. We are never off the clock. As long as we are away from our homeland (heaven), we must be busy representing the good news of Christ to this world.

Some people with whom you come in contact every day need to know about Jesus. Some of them are watching you and waiting for you to tell them about Him. As you go through this day, list the people with whom you come in contact.

_____

_____

_____

_____

_____

Of those people identify at least three and begin to pray for them. Ask God to help you find a way to dialogue with them about spiritual things.

1._____

2._____

3._____

Add the names to the prayer section of "My FAITH Connections" (p. 23) and ask your prayer partners to begin praying for them as well. (You may not want to share full names.)

DAY 5

The writer of Proverbs declared that

> The plans of the diligent certainly lead to profit,
> but anyone who is reckless only becomes poor (Prov. 21:5).

God wants to do important work in your life, your church, and your community. Some of these things can happen through your involvement in FAITH training.

In Yourself

At the end of session 1 we met Kathy, who explained the difference FAITH made in her life. Review her story on page 22. There have been and continue to be changes in Kathy's life as she continues to place herself in a position to be used by God.

During session 1 you were asked to dream about what you hope to gain by being involved in FAITH training (p. 19). By now you have had time to think more about it. Write three goals or changes you hope to see in yourself over the next 12 weeks.
1._____
2._____
3._____

In Your Church

You and others involved in FAITH training will make a difference in your church. Think about what it could mean for your church if every person on a FAITH team shared with at least one person about Jesus.

What would happen in your church if every week at least one person accepted Christ?
_____

How would it change your worship? _____
_____

As you think about your church, list three things you hope will happen as a result of FAITH training over the next 12 weeks.
1._____
2._____
3._____

In Your Community

Take time to drive around your community, including the area around your church. Take it all in. What did you observe?

What are three things you hope will happen in your community over the next 12 weeks?
1._____
2._____
3._____

Ask God to bring about these nine changes. Thank Him in advance for the victories.

MY FAITH JOURNEY

SESSION

MOVING TOWARD SPIRITUAL DIALOGUE

SESSION GOALS

You will—
- discover actions that can lead to spiritual dialogues;
- practice asking open-ended questions;
- understand and be able to share your Sunday School testimony;
- develop and refine your evangelistic story;
- identify responses to the Key Question;
- discover the importance of maintaining a passion for God.

Describe your hometown. What makes it unique? Is there something special a person must see when visiting?

_____

_____

_____

Most of us could write a book about our hometowns. Asking about someone's hometown is a simple question, but it is loaded with possible insights into the person's life. The next time you fly, listen to the people around you. Most conversations start about where a person is going or originally came from.

It's amazing that complete strangers share details about themselves when they fly on an airplane. You will hear all kinds of things—including information coming from your mouth that you haven't even told your next-door neighbor! Maybe we should replace all the chairs in our Sunday School classes with airline seats so that people will talk to one another. The magazines in the backs of the seats would be replaced by Bibles and Sunday School resources. Can't you just see the possibilities?

Don't you wish talking about spiritual things were as easy as that conversation about your hometown or as comfortable as the dialogues taking place on airplanes? How can we naturally introduce spiritual matters into a conversation?

Jesus is your greatest _____ _____ for initiating and directing spiritual conversations. He did it in everyday life as He encountered people doing normal things. He used a compliment to dialogue with a religious leader (see John 3). He asked a woman standing at a well whether she would like to drink from a well that would always quench her thirst (see John 4). He asked a sick man if he wanted to get well (see John 5). Some of these seem like obvious questions, but Jesus was _____ in His approach. He was looking for the opportunity to talk about more than teaching, water, or health. He was looking for an opportunity to engage in spiritual dialogue, staying attuned to His Father's voice all the time.

LOOKING FOR OPPORTUNITIES

_____ in _____ with the Father enabled Jesus to identify the person's true spiritual need. Because He lives in you, you can listen with His compassion and spiritual insight as you talk with lost people.

How could the following situations open doors to introduce spiritual dialogue?
• You are talking with other parents while watching your child's soccer game.
  One parent asks if you go to church.

_____

_____

_____

_____

- *While you are eating out, your waiter appears to be preoccupied with something other than work. You ask if you can include him in your blessing, and he asks you if you can keep a secret.*

_____

_____

_____

_____

- *At work the person at the desk next to you mentions that he has just started reading a book. You discover that it is a book you have as well but have not yet read.*

_____

_____

_____

_____

Each of these opportunities could lead a person into spiritual dialogue. The situations described represent the multitude of _____ we have all around us if we would stop long enough to notice. These encounters are part of everyday life. We can ignore them, or we can enjoy the _____ _____ God has placed in our lives.

Not all of these contacts are incidental. We can intentionally _____ _____ in positions where we can have dialogue with lost people. Coaching a sports team, joining a civic club, and inviting an unchurched person to join you and other believers for lunch are all actions that lead to lifestyle opportunities for witnessing.

Regardless of the origin of the opportunity, intentional or divinely directed, you can take the initiative to move a conversation toward spiritual matters. As you interact with people, look for the following things that will help you initiate spiritual dialogue.

1. Search for common areas of _____.

One way to keep your gospel presentation from being impersonal is to make sure you genuinely talk about common interests. Rarely will you visit or interact for long with someone with whom you have nothing in common. A good listener capitalizes on these areas of interest by _____ to _____ the person God created.

2. Keep an inquisitive _____.

Listening skills improve if you treat the person as a new adventure. The person God has brought into your life is a treasure in God's eyes. _____ _____ with genuine curiosity as you search for the many qualities that make this person special.

3. Listen for what the person already knows about _____ _____.

It is important that you discover ways lost persons are _____. Have they already attended church? Did someone invite them, and if so, what is their relationship to that person? Have they been to Sunday School or another small group? How did they describe that experience? Did they come to a special event? Do they already know people in your church?

4. Discover details about a person's _____ _____.

You can discover helpful information about the person's spiritual condition by the way that person views past church _____. Were these relationships positive or negative? Does the person have realistic ideals for a church? Has he or she been hurt in the past? If so, what does this hurt tell you about the person?

5. Let your friend _____.

If you let people talk, they will eventually reveal some _____. Is he bored with life? Does she have any complaints? Are they dealing with a conflict? What are their fears? Does your new acquaintance express guilt, regret, or anger? You have a message of hope for people who struggle, so be sensitive to needs as they begin to surface.

6. Ask for _____.

If you are uncertain about what someone is saying, _____ _____ for clarification. (This point will be particularly important as you learn how to ask the Key Question.) Asking questions shows that you are interested. Do not interrogate or accuse. For example, instead of asking, "Is that why you stopped coming to church?" you might ask, "How did that situation affect you?"

Think about your conversations over the past three days. Identify conversations that included any of the six features described above. Did you take advantage of the opportunity to ask about spiritual things? ☐ Yes ☐ No

What other questions could you have asked in those conversations to move toward dialogue about spiritual things?

_____

_____

_____

TWO SKILLS TO MASTER

Two basic conversational skills will help you move toward spiritual dialogue when you talk with lost people.

1. Ask _____ _____.

An open-ended question is one that requires more than a yes-or-no answer. Such questions usually call for answers that reveal feelings, thoughts, and impressions, as opposed to simple facts. Too many times we can kill a conversation by asking closed questions.

How could the following issues be addressed by asking open-ended questions? Reword each question to make it open-ended.

Do you attend church? _____

_____

Did you know anyone in our class? _____

_____

Do you have any questions about our church? _____

_____

A good way to begin an open-ended question is to say, "Tell me about … ," which allows the person to elaborate and clarify. As people share more about themselves, they give you more potential places to connect and direct the conversation toward deeper issues. By asking follow-up questions (also open-ended) that point to deeper issues, you can move toward a conversation about salvation.

2. Let people tell their _____.

We all like to talk about ourselves, and we will if given the opportunity. Most of us are starved for intelligent conversation, especially when we are the centerpiece of that conversation! Too many times the conversation focuses on us and our thoughts, and we forget that the other person has thoughts and experiences too.

While your ultimate goal is to dialogue about the salvation we have discovered, don't ignore the multitude of potential problems and life issues the person may face. By dealing with expressed problems and life issues, you might earn someone's trust and the privilege of sharing Jesus.

None of us know all God has planned, so we must pay attention and walk through the open doors He places in front of us.

SPECIAL TOOLS TO INCORPORATE IN A CONVERSATION

1. Your Sunday School/small-group _____
- "In our Sunday School class we have made so many friends our age with the same needs and problems. We share and pray for one another, especially about marriage and family issues. We keep praying all week and often e-mail one another when we know someone needs support or encouragement. On Sundays we share answers to prayer and other needs. Sometimes we hear from our teacher during the week."
- "Our leader has been where we are and encourages us to see the way God wants us to live. He's a great Bible teacher, but we all have a responsibility to learn God's Word together."
- "We do enjoyable things with our Sunday School class all the time—dinner or coffee together, once-a-month fellowships, baby showers, and all kinds of church activities. In fact, this Saturday is a women's luncheon. We'll come pick you up if you can go with us. And we'll meet you in the parking lot on Sunday morning and take you to our Sunday School class."

These experiences all reflect a Sunday School class or a small group that is meeting the needs of its members. The people attending are satisfied customers. On day 2 of "My FAITH Journey" this week, you will write your Sunday School testimony. A Sunday School testimony is not a salvation testimony; rather, it gives you a tool to connect with others by sharing how a group of Christ-followers has helped meet needs in your journey of faith.

In general, the following benefits are likely to be reflected in your Sunday School testimony. Relate the benefit that most applies to you; don't try to share all of them. Remember, your Sunday School testimony is dynamic, so it may reflect different benefits at different times. There may be more benefits, but these tend to be the most common:

- _____ and _____. Give a specific example of support you receive and friendships (new or long-term) you have developed through your class or department.
- _____ *in times of need*. Tell about an experience when class members assisted you.
- *Opportunities to learn and apply* _____ _____. Describe benefits of Bible study in the class.
- _____ *as a Christian*. Identify ways you have grown as a Christian through experiences in or through your Bible-study group.
- *An opportunity to make a* _____ *in others' lives*. Describe how you make a difference in the lives of others by serving in your Sunday School class.

As you develop your Sunday School testimony, focus on the general benefits of Sunday School and current experience that reflects those benefits. As you dialogue with others in your daily life and on FAITH visits, you will find that your Sunday School testimony is a source of encouragement to those who want to be a part of a small group that cares for and supports one another.

2. Your evangelistic _____

Many of us could spend hours sharing our faith story. But when making a visit, we normally have a limited amount of time to share. It is important to know how to communicate only significant highlights.

On day 3 of last week's "My FAITH Journey," you were asked to write your evangelistic story (p. 26). Review what you wrote as we examine the evangelistic story. As you recall from this assignment, we used the following outline to help you share the highlights of your evangelistic story.

- *Preconversion experience.* Select a time in your life that illustrates what it was like without the assurance of _____. Many lost people can relate to experiences such as feelings of loneliness, fear, guilt, and the lack of purpose in life. Many can relate more to these experiences than they can to being saved and accepting Christ. Be as _____ as possible so that another person can relate to your preconversion experience. Keep this part of the story to _____ _____ or less.

    If you became a believer when you were young, first of all, be thankful. God most likely spared you a great deal of heartache and regret. Second, focus on what you wanted or what caused you to want to make a commitment. You may point to the faith of your family, things happening in your life, or discoveries you made as part of a Bible study group.

    Because none of us are born as believers, we all have a preconversion experience. It may not have been dramatic, but God is more interested in the truth than in the dramatic.

- *Conversion experience.* You may want to use the statement "____ _____ ____ _____ _____" to describe your conversion. This statement is helpful because it expresses the fact that your life was changed without telling, at this point, the details. Soon you will ask the Key Question, and you want to know what the other person thinks. If you tell someone exactly how you were saved before you begin to dialogue seriously about spiritual matters, then in essence you are sharing the answer to the way a person goes to heaven. The person could merely repeat your answer.

  The purpose of the evangelistic story is to create a _____ in the person to know _____ to have heaven. You want to whet the person's appetite. This part of your testimony should consist of this one statement only.

- *Recent benefits of conversion.* Share statements and _____ _____ that reflect God's _____ in your life. You are sharing evidence of your assurance of heaven. Close your testimony with a statement of _____, such as "I know if I died tonight, I would spend eternity in heaven." This part of your evangelistic story should be less than _____ _____.

*Reread what you wrote on page 26. As you develop your evangelistic story, try to use words unchurched people understand rather than including phrases like **born again** to describe your experience.*

THE KEY QUESTION

When trying to initiate meaningful dialogue about spiritual matters, remember that the most important spiritual matter is a person's relationship with Jesus. You are seeking to find a way to introduce discussion about _____. With the Holy Spirit's guidance you can introduce this kind of dialogue by asking the _____ _____—a _____ question that asks for an _____, opening the door for dialogue and, hopefully, the FAITH gospel presentation.

The Key Question we use is this: *In your personal opinion, what do you understand it takes for a person to get to heaven and have eternal life?* This question can give rise to other questions about spiritual things, but it serves as the launching pad for the FAITH _____ _____.

The way a person answers the Key Question dictates how you proceed. He or she can give you one of four types of answers: faith, works, unclear, or no opinion.

1. A _____ answer

A faith answer indicates an understanding and a personal acceptance that only by trusting Jesus as Savior and Lord can someone experience eternity and heaven. If someone responds with a faith answer, ask the person to share the way he or she came to know the grace of God's forgiveness. For example, you might comment, "That's what the Bible teaches. What circumstances led you to that experience?" This can be a good place to ask about church relationships. You will want to ask because someone may know the answer but has not yet made a commitment to Jesus. Some cult groups give what appears to be a faith answer; yet what they mean by *Jesus* is different from the Jesus revealed in Scripture. If the person is a believer, affirm the response and celebrate together as fellow Christians.

2. A _____ answer

Many people think if they live a good life by doing good things or at least avoiding serious offenses, they will be rewarded with heaven. However, the Bible teaches that no one can earn salvation. Some postmodern adults especially give no thought at all to heaven but are concerned with day-to-day issues of hope, relationships, and security. Ultimately, keep in mind that your team offers hope as it shares good news about a personal relationship with Jesus.

It may not happen often, but when someone tells you, "I don't believe in heaven," it will be helpful to probe for more information. You or your team leader might respond, "Of course, it's your decision not to believe in heaven, but what do you understand the *Bible* teaches about how a person can enter heaven and have eternal life?" In almost every case the person will revert to a works answer. Then to ask, "May I share with you what the Bible has to say?" becomes a natural transition that can allow the conversation to continue.

In general, when you detect a works answer, be particularly sensitive; the Lord may have given you an opportunity to share the gospel. As already suggested, you may need to probe for more information to better understand their response; for example, "Which of the Ten Commandments do you find the hardest to keep?" "Why do you think going to church is so important?" "When you read the Bible, what is your favorite part?"

You will eventually want to state something like this: "Actually, [person's name], that is one answer many people give. I'd like to share with you what I've discovered in the Bible about that question, if I may."

3. An _____ answer

An unclear answer is one that does not readily indicate the person's spiritual condition. For example, a person might say, "I love God" or "I believe in God." If a response is unclear, gently ask for more explanation. For example, you might ask, "[Person's name], I think I know what you mean, but would you tell me more?"

4. _____ opinion

A person may say he or she has no opinion. Such a response may indicate a lack of interest or an inability to express his or her thoughts. For example, someone may express, "I don't believe in heaven." In these conversations try to clarify responses by asking if the person thinks about eternity and spiritual things.

MAKING THE TRANSITION

Hopefully, with an unsaved person you will be able to make a _____ to the gospel presentation by saying, "I'd like to share with you what I discovered in the Bible about that question if it is all right." If the person says no, graciously thank him or her for allowing you to get to know him or her. By your response leave the door open for _____ _____. Invite him or her to attend Sunday School, another small group, a worship service, or a special event with you. Determine whether the person is open to being involved in a Bible study group, seeking to enroll him or her if possible. Offer to pray for the person, remembering any needs or requests that he or she expressed earlier in the conversation.

If the person expresses an interest in knowing how the Bible answers the Key Question, continue. You want the presentation to be part of a natural conversation. You may want to say something like "There is a word that can be used to answer this question: *FAITH* [spell out on fingers]" or "In the Bible I discovered five truths that answered that question for me."

Be _____ when making this transition. Don't attack the person's answer. You asked for their opinion, and opinions are personal. They have shared what they have discovered in life, and now you are asking permission to share what you have discovered.

What are some ways you could make a transition from listening to a response to the Key Question to sharing the FAITH gospel presentation?

_____

_____

_____

_____

WHEN MAKING A HOME VISIT

When making a home visit, you can take certain actions to help you open spiritual dialogue with the residents, particularly if you do not know them.

- Look for _____ about the family when you arrive, such as toys for a specific age or gender, university parking stickers, and items used for hobbies.
- Identify yourself as being from your _____.
- Make sure you know the _____ _____ of the person to whom you are speaking.
- Introduce the _____ _____ visiting with you.
- _____ the reason you are making this visit. For example, this statement might be appropriate: "You were a guest in our Sunday School yesterday, and we wanted to give you the opportunity to get to know us better." Using a question like this can put a person at ease and take him off the defensive.
- _____ _____ in the things important to the person(s) being visited.
- As often as possible and appropriate, call persons by _____.

Accepting outsiders into the home is increasingly less acceptable in our society, particularly if people think we want to sell them something or put pressure on them. Therefore, it is important to be at ease personally and to make the individuals being visited feel _____. Because you are on someone else's turf, you should respect every aspect of their _____ and _____. You may or may not be given an audience, but keep the door open for future efforts. While failing to go guarantees that we will have no audience, failing to treat others with respect guarantees that we will have no audience in the days ahead.

Day 4 of last week's "My FAITH Journey" asked you to identify persons with whom you already have contact and who need to know Jesus (p. 27). How could you use the information in this session to initiate dialogue with these persons about spiritual things?

_____

_____

_____

_____

GETTING BEYOND THE CITY LIMITS

We began this session by listing characteristics of our hometowns. It's easy for most of us to talk about our hometowns, our families, the colleges we attend or attended, our favorite sports teams, our hobbies, or our jobs. It's always easy to talk about the things and people we love.

Could one reason we have difficulty sharing Jesus with others be that we have lost our _____ for Him? Could it be that we have grown lukewarm toward Him and have forgotten what it was like to be head over heels in love with God? Do we perhaps need to renew our vows to God and reignite our passion for Him?

The Bible frequently compares our relationship with God to a marriage. Hosea compared his wife's unfaithfulness to Israel's unfaithfulness to God (see Hos. 2). Jesus is called the Bridegroom, and the church is called His bride (see Rev. 21:9). God expects us to have a _____ _____ with Him, one that is alive and growing. Then we will always be ready to _____ about Him and what He has done for us.

What are you doing to keep your passion for God fresh and alive?

_____

_____

_____

_____

What do you need to do to fan the flames and regain your passion for God?

_____

_____

_____

_____

MY FAITH CONNECTIONS

Visitation Summary

Attempts _____
Completed visits _____
Key Question asked _____

Record a synopsis of your team's visits. Include actions you may need to take on needs discovered. Whom should you tell about these needs? Prayer partners? Sunday School teacher? Minister?

_____

_____

_____

_____

Life-Witness Summary

Key Question asked _____

_____

_____

_____

_____

My Journey This Week

What has God taught you this week? Record insights you have gained about God and yourself.

_____

_____

_____

_____

To-Do List

- ☐ Read session 2
- ☐ Completed "My FAITH Journey":
  - ☐ Day 1
  - ☐ Day 2
  - ☐ Day 3
  - ☐ Day 4
  - ☐ Day 5

- ☐ Completed Sunday School testimony
- ☐ Contacted prayer partners
- ☐ Continued to memorize FAITH presentation
- ☐ _____
- ☐ _____
- ☐ _____
- ☐ _____
- ☐ _____
- ☐ _____

Prayer List

Lost people for whom you are praying:
- ☐ _____
- ☐ _____
- ☐ _____
- ☐ _____
- ☐ _____
- ☐ _____
- ☐ _____
- ☐ _____
- ☐ _____
- ☐ _____
- ☐ _____
- ☐ _____

Others needing prayer:
- ☐ _____
- ☐ _____
- ☐ _____
- ☐ _____
- ☐ _____
- ☐ _____
- ☐ _____
- ☐ _____
- ☐ _____
- ☐ _____

DAY 1

Jacob was in love with Rachel. To prove it, he was willing to work for seven years for his future father-in-law. When he was tricked into taking Leah, Rachel's older sister, as his wife, Jacob was willing to work for another seven years for the right to take Rachel's hand in marriage as well (see Gen. 29). There was no question about Jacob's love for Rachel. She knew he loved her. Everyone around knew that Jacob loved Rachel. He had proved his love through 14 years of service to her father, and he continued to demonstrate his love for her after the 14 years had ended.

We may not be called on to work for 14 years to prove that we love someone, but we nonetheless demonstrate our love to people. Think about the three persons you love the most. How do they know that you love them?

_____

_____

_____

Jesus and the 11 disciples (Judas had hanged himself) were sitting on the shore after Jesus' resurrection. He had prepared breakfast for them, and they had just finished the meal. Jesus turned to Peter and asked him a startling question—not just once but three times: "Do you love Me more than these?" We don't know who *these* were—perhaps the other disciples or Peter's fishing buddies. Did he love them more than he loved Jesus? Did he love Jesus more than he loved his friends? Peter had denied knowing Jesus during the crucifixion. Now Jesus asked Peter about his love for Him. How could Peter prove his love for Jesus? Peter had just lost three opportunities to prove it (see John 21:15-18).

If that had been you sitting on that shore that morning, what would you have said, and how would you have proved your love for Jesus?

_____

_____

_____

Jesus gave Peter two actions to prove his love. The first was to take care of the other followers of Jesus. The second was to give his life as a sacrifice for Jesus. In a way Jesus was telling Peter he would have another opportunity to prove his love for Him, and this time he would not fail.

Jesus continues to give His followers opportunities to demonstrate their love for Him. Christianity is not about rituals and keeping laws; it is about an intimate love relationship between God and us. Love always expresses itself.

Throughout this day look for ways you can demonstrate your love for God. To remind yourself of the importance of keeping that love relationship alive, review "Getting Beyond the City Limits" on page 38. Note things you may need to change to continue developing your relationship with God. Ask God to help you demonstrate your love for Him today.

DAY 2

Sunday School is an important part of your church. It is where friendships are made, questions are answered, and needs are discovered and met.

In each category below describe one way Sunday School has made a difference in your life. You may want to refer to page 34 to better understand each category.

• *Friends and support:* _____

_____

• *Help in times of need:* _____

_____

• *Opportunities to learn and apply God's Word:* _____

_____

• *Growth as a Christian:* _____

_____

• *An opportunity to make a difference in others' lives:* _____

_____

Place a check mark beside the category that is the most significant to you. Why did you choose the one you did?

_____

_____

As you look at what you recorded, think about the lost persons whose names you wrote on your prayer list. Which of your answers would most appeal to them?

_____

How could you use your experiences to encourage them to join you for Sunday School?

_____

_____

Identify one person on your prayer list with whom you can share your Sunday School testimony in the next 24 hours. Ask God to give you courage to share with him or her.

DAY 3

Second Kings 7:3-11 records the account of four men with a skin disease, desperate men who faced a sure death. If they stayed in their city, they would starve. If they went to the enemy camp, they would most likely be executed. Because their disease was incurable, they were going to die anyway and had very little to lose either way. They took a chance and went to the enemy's camp with the hope that they would find mercy there.

When they arrived, a surprise awaited them. The night before they arrived, God had caused the enemy to hear what they thought was an approaching army. They had fled, leaving behind everything—clothes, food, and money. When the four lepers arrived, they had free access to everything. They had a big party—or at least as big a party as four men with leprosy can have. Realizing that their discovery could save their city, they returned to tell the city leaders about the enemy's flight. At first no one believed them. However, after their story was confirmed, the townspeople rushed to the abandoned camp, and the city was saved. These men were heroes because they were willing to share what they had discovered.

The interesting part of the story is that the men thought they were risking it all when they left to approach the enemy. They had no idea that God had gone ahead of them and was doing what only He can do.

At times we may think that by sharing with a friend or relative, we are risking it all. We forget that God is always at work doing what only He can do. Yesterday you may have discovered that reality when you shared your Sunday School testimony with another person. You may discover it today as you encounter a person needing your help. You may be standing in line at the supermarket and find yourself in a position to encourage another person, share about your Sunday School class, or dialogue about spiritual things.

We see the risk, while God sees what He has been doing. The only way we will see what He is doing is by going. As we go, we will discover, like the four lepers, that God is up to something.

Thinking back over the past few weeks, how have you seen God at work in and around you?

_____

_____

_____

_____

How does knowing that God is at work encourage you? _____

_____

_____

_____

Thank God for being alive and active in this world.

DAY 4

The Key Question is designed to help you engage in meaningful spiritual dialogue in a nonthreatening way.

Write the Key Question here. _____

_____

Imagine you have just asked someone the Key Question, and the person responds in one of the following ways. How would you respond? What additional questions could you ask? If you need help, refer to "The Key Question," beginning on page 35.

- *"That's a hard question but a good one. You really need to ask that question to my neighbor next door. He enjoys philosophical debates and tells me about different books he is reading about religions. He could give you a good answer."*

How would you respond? _____

_____

What additional questions could you ask? _____

_____

- *"I can't believe you would ask such a simple question. Everyone knows the answer to that. You mentioned part of it when you talked about your Sunday School class. You get to heaven by attending church, loving God, and obeying the commands in the Bible and other writings."*

How would you respond? _____

_____

What additional questions could you ask? _____

_____

- *"In my opinion, there are many ways to get to heaven. Every religion is about the same, and each has its own strengths and weaknesses. The issue is being consistent with what you believe and letting God sort out the details. He's a fair God and will be more than fair when we get there. You're not going to tell me I'm wrong, are you?"*

How would you respond? _____

_____

What additional questions could you ask? _____

_____

DAY 5

In the previous session we learned that Jesus was the master at initiating conversations with lost and searching people. Look at John 4:7-26. In approaching the woman at the well, Jesus did at least three things that can help us initiate spiritual dialogue as well.

1. *Jesus used a simple approach.* He began by asking for a drink of water. How simple is that? His approach wasn't complicated or filled with philosophical debate. The woman had the cup, and he asked for a drink. Most of us make starting a conversation too difficult: *How will I introduce myself? What if they are selfish with their water? How will I impress them with my knowledge of water and wells?* Jesus just asked for a drink.

2. *Jesus asked for something natural.* Thirst is something we all experience. We have it every day. It would be natural for a person to ask for a drink in the middle of the afternoon in a dry desert. How else could a person begin a conversation? He didn't ask her for a shovel or an ax. It was obvious that she had a pail of water and could provide a drink.

3. *Jesus changed the focus from His need to her needs.* We don't know whether Jesus got a drink. The Bible doesn't tell us. But we know that the woman was spiritually thirsty, and Jesus focused on her need and not His own. She became the focal point. Too many times we don't allow the other person to be the focal point of the conversation. Jesus shared the limelight so that He could meet the woman's spiritual needs.

How would you put into a single sentence the principles Jesus used to begin a conversation?

_____

_____

_____

When talking with the woman at the well, Jesus found a connecting point. Connecting points are critical places where we can begin to move a conversation toward needs and spiritual concerns. Jesus gave us one example of how to connect with people.

Review the names of the persons for whom you are praying. How can you connect with them, following Jesus' example?

_____

_____

_____

_____

In the next session we will discover ways we can connect with people the way Jesus did. Ask God to help you connect with others in intentional, genuine ways.

SESSION

FINDING CONNECTION POINTS

SESSION GOALS

You will—
- identify the five types of FAITH team visits;
- outline general actions to take when visiting;
- identify steps for conducting an Opinion Poll;
- discover intentional actions for fostering relationships with lost people;
- define success in witnessing.

When Paul wrote his letters to various churches, he usually added a personal note at the end that included names. Sometimes he had kind things to say, and other times he warned his readers to shun certain people. Have you ever wondered whether, if you had been Paul's friend, he would have included you in one of his letters? If so, would he have said something kind? What Kingdom accomplishment in your life would he have highlighted?

At the end of the first letter to the Corinthians, Paul named three persons—Stephanas, Fortunatus, and Achaicus—who are forever remembered. Their role was simple: they made a ministry visit of sorts to Paul. The Corinthian church had sent them to care for Paul, representing the church's interests and concerns. Paul remembered them as people who "refreshed my spirit" (1 Cor. 16:18). In today's vernacular we would say they were a breath of fresh air. If we read between the lines, we get the sense that these men acted as an expression of God's love. They made a difference in someone's life by making a personal visit.

By making visits, we have opportunities to make this same kind of impact. For us the issue is finding a way to _____ with people, intersecting their lives for the purpose of representing God's love and concern. We do this intentionally by initiating spiritual dialogues as we make assigned FAITH visits, conduct Opinion Polls, and build day-to-day relationships.

There's a lot to think about this week. Don't forget that in assigned FAITH visits and Opinion Polls, your _____ _____ takes the lead until you are ready. Don't hesitate to ask questions as you observe, pray, and interact with people in visits and in daily-life encounters.

PREPARING FOR A VISIT

You may be called to visit someone for a variety of reasons. Someone may have requested a contact, a friend may have submitted names, or members may have suddenly become inactive. No matter what kind of visit you are going to make, your team can take some general steps to prepare.

1. Gather as much _____ as possible before going out.
If possible, find out whether someone is a member of a Sunday School class or a small group; if so, look for attendance patterns. Try to learn the source of the request as well. Team members should share with one another what they already know about the situation or family. This is not a gossip time, so share only facts that are of value.

2. Establish the _____ of your visit.
By establishing a specific purpose for the visit, you can then focus on why you are there and can make sure you deal with the issue or issues identified. The purpose of the visit serves as a means to keep the visit on track.

Some visits are _____ _____. Your team is there to find out how and what ministry needs to take place. Finding out why a person has suddenly become inactive may be part of this process. Your goal would then be to find the information needed so that future ministry could be done.

Your team may be going to initiate some _____ _____. During this type of visit, your goal is to determine ministry actions that could be taken to help the individual. In these cases the specific need has already been identified, and now you seek to put a plan of action into place.

In another visit your team may simply be called on to _____
_____ and His _____. You may be going in response to a known death,
other need, or another difficult situation.

3. Designate a _____ _____.
He or she will lead the dialogue during the visit.

MAKING A VISIT
Follow these general principles when making the visit.

**1. Always begin by _____ yourself
and your team members.**
Also identify your church and tell them why you are visiting. Be honest and direct.
The purpose you identified prior to arriving should be reflected in what you say.

**2. As you begin your conversation, seek to _____
information you have been given.**
Here are a few examples of ways to validate information.
- *If suddenly inactive.* "We noticed that at one time you were active in our Sunday
  School class. We were concerned and wanted to invite you to be part of class
  on Sunday."
- *If a referral.* "[Give referral name] is a member of our church and asked that we
  stop by. They have shared with us that [identify situation], and we wanted to
  learn whether we could help and pray with you."
- *If an anonymous referral.* You may want to approach the visit as an Opinion Poll
  (see pp. 50–51) and transition into the purpose of the visit by asking if you could
  pray for them after the Opinion Poll is complete. Be sensitive to the reality that
  this might be an evangelistic opportunity.

3. As you ask questions, _____.
Remember that you want to let people tell their stories. A word of caution: if the
person begins to criticize the church or specific individuals, listen but do not agree
with criticisms. By agreeing with them, you may run the risk of validating their
rationale for no longer attending.

**4. As they share, explore ways your team can _____
personal connections.**
Ministry generally takes place as people are connected with other people. Seek
to find ways people in your class or on your team could be part of the solution or
could provide support. Be sensitive to the person's feelings by asking permission to
take specific actions at this point.

5. End all visits by offering to _____.
This step is critical in keeping the door open for future ministry. Ask how they
would like for you to pray and be sensitive to their comments. The way you pray
may be the most significant thing that takes place during this visit.

6. _____ the visit in the car.
Each team member may have a different perspective and may remember different
details that were shared. Use the following questions to guide your discussion.

- What needs did we discover?
- Whom do we need to notify about these needs?
- How can we be part of the solution?
- What can we do better the next time we make a visit like this one?

Do not sit in the car in front of the residence to debrief!

7. _____ what you said you would do.
If you made any promises during the visit, keep them. Your credibility is on the line. Keeping your promise may be just what is needed to bring the once-active-but-now-inactive person back into the fellowship of the church. In the same way, those who are facing difficulties are counting on you to come through for them.

List the steps to take when making a visit.

1. _____

2. _____

3. _____

4. _____

5. _____

6. _____

7. _____

TYPES OF FAITH VISITS
There are five types of FAITH visits.

1. An _____ visit
An evangelistic visit is made to anyone whose spiritual condition you do not know. They may have been a first-time guest the previous Sunday or may have attended a special church event. A Sunday School member may have asked that a FAITH team visit a friend. The purpose of this kind of visit is to initiate _____ about spiritual matters; discover the person's _____ _____; and if the opportunity arises, share the FAITH _____ _____.

2. A _____ visit
A follow-up visit is an additional visit to someone you have already met. The person may want to talk more about the gospel presentation. She may not have had time during a previous visit but has time to talk now. The individual may have made a decision for Christ and may need encouragement to take the next steps.

Remember that Jesus commissioned us to make disciples, not mere converts. After a person accepts Christ, he or she needs additional attention and care. If your team has led someone to Christ, you have the privilege and responsibility to help that new believer learn to _____ as a _____. We will discuss this kind of visit in more detail in session 10.

3. A _____ visit

You've probably noticed that baptism is a type of visit on your team Weekly Participation Report. We will consider this special type of follow-up in session 10. The same team that has the privilege of leading someone to Christ helps the new Christian begin to grow in _____ and _____.

4. A _____ visit

A Sunday School or small-group ministry visit is made to someone who is already a _____ of Sunday School or a small group. Just as you will discover some evangelistic visits to be divine appointments, Sunday School ministry visits can also be timely both for you and for the persons you visit. In some cases good ministry creates a catalyst for unchurched individuals to _____ to Sunday School in the first place. A ministry visit may also be the point at which a member _____ to Sunday School. Ultimately, some of these connections result in a person's making a decision for Christ.

Just because a person is on a Sunday School roll, you cannot assume he or she has made a commitment to Christ. Ask the Key Question even to persons enrolled in Sunday School. If they are believers, you will have the opportunity to hear about and celebrate their conversion. If they are not, you will have another opportunity to share Jesus with someone.

Ministry visits are most often made to absentees, nonattenders (persons on roll but not attending; for all practical purposes they are inactive in Sunday School), and members with special life needs (illness, hospitalization, death in the family, counseling need, and so forth). As noted previously, you will want to gather as much information as possible before going in order to understand the purpose of your visit.

- *Ministry visits to* _____. When visiting an absentee, you are most likely trying to keep that person from becoming a chronic absentee or an inactive member. In such a visit, address the person's absence in a positive manner. Be truthful as you say how much the individual has been missed. Describe the exciting things that are happening. Take along current Bible study or leisure-reading material if the absence was on a Sunday when new material was distributed. Bring the person up-to-date on churchwide events.

  If the person expresses something negative, thank the person for being open and honest. Again, don't agree with negative statements about the church or its ministry. By all means listen politely and commit to pray for the situation.

- *Ministry visits to* _____. Nonattenders are persons on your Sunday School roll you have never seen or who have not been seen in a long time. In such a visit, the person may not know you, so it will resemble an evangelistic visit. Sunday School testimonies would be beneficial. Take along information that may help the person reconnect.

  Some may see maintaining contact with nonattenders as a waste of time, because so few appear to ever return to the church. It can be discouraging if this is the only group you focus on. You don't know when people will need the church, but sooner or later, they will. Deaths, serious illness, and many other life events or crises will cause even the strongest critics to seek God. By maintaining some kind of contact with every person on a Sunday School roll, you keep the door open for ministry.

- *Ministry visits to persons with special* _____ _____. Contacting persons who experience a special life event—surgery, hospitalization, birth of a baby, and so forth—can keep them in touch with their Sunday School class and the class in touch with their needs. Usually, teams will know the nature of the need before arriving at the home, but sometimes needs become apparent during a visit. These visits do not necessarily need to be long, but the length depends on the identified purpose of the visit. Do what you need to do to accomplish the purpose and be on your way.

Be sure to share the results of ministry visits with the Sunday School teacher or small-group leader.

5. An _____ _____ visit

When you were first asked to participate in FAITH training, you probably became excited about the possibility of sharing the gospel with and ministering to persons assigned to your Sunday School department or class or to your small group. You may feel more comfortable visiting your peers than visiting people you have never met or about whom you have no information. Then you heard about the Opinion Poll.

Most FAITH learners are apprehensive about the Opinion Poll until they see it work. Likely, your FAITH team members will feel just as uneasy until they see how God uses people to _____ _____ with this simple tool. The Opinion Poll gives your FAITH team some important bridge-building experiences and opportunities.

As with all visits, Opinion Poll visits are a _____ _____. Team members pray for one another, and they take different responsibilities during the visit. Teams should follow these guidelines in making Opinion Poll visits.

1. Prior to approaching the house, make sure the following _____ have been assigned to team members.
   - The _____ will knock, introduce the team by first name only, and identify your church. He or she will be the team member actually conducting the survey.
   - The _____ will record responses on the survey form.
   - Someone will _____ for the spokesperson and tactfully take care of distractions that may occur, such as those caused by pets and children.
2. When approaching a house, your team members should have pleasant expressions on their faces. As your team approaches the door, the spokesperson is prepared to state the _____ of this brief survey: to help our church be more responsive to needs in our community. The team requests _____ to ask the person a few questions. If permission is given, the spokesperson asks the first question on the survey.
3. Team members listen for clues about spiritual needs or _____, talk about interests and church _____, and follow up on responses to the Key Question. If someone gives a faith answer, rejoice with him and invite him to tell you about that decision. If he gives a works, unclear, or no-opinion response, ask permission to share what you have discovered in the Bible.
4. If the person declines, be _____ and _____. Offer to pray with her and quickly let her know about any upcoming church events that may interest her. If she says yes, share the FAITH gospel presentation with her.
5. At the conclusion of the visit, always offer to _____ for the person and for anyone else who lives there. This is one way to discover potential ministry needs and to keep the door open for future ministry.
6. Once the survey is complete, the recorder should _____ as much information as possible about the person or family, including name, address, approximate age, and follow-up opportunities. The team member responsible for recording information may need to write rapidly, so he or she may need to

rewrite comments on a second form so that it can be read and the appropriate follow-up actions can be taken.

Now for a dose of Opinion Poll reality: it will not always go the way it is supposed to go. Here are some ideas that may help you deal with challenges.

- *If someone is not at home.* Many people will not be at home. Simply leave a note on the door or a publication from your church. If a no-solicitation sign is on the property, respect the request and do not leave anything behind.
- *If the individual does not want to participate.* Some will not permit you to begin a conversation. Always be cordial and respectful. If a person chooses not to participate in the Opinion Poll, be gracious. Note all information discovered—even refusals—on the Opinion Poll form.
- *If the person has time to answer only the first two questions.* Even if someone provides partial or incomplete information, he or she may represent a prospect or a prospect family for your church.
- *If he or she asks what will happen with the recorded information.* Some will want to know that what they are doing is of value. State that your church wants to know the needs and interests of people around the church. Church leaders will examine all recorded information and will consider it in future planning.
- *If someone responds in an antagonistic fashion.* Some people will be unpleasant. These are the 5 percent identified by Thom Rainer as antagonistic. Once again, be cordial and respectful. Remember that one of your goals is to establish an open door for the future that was once closed. A kind word may be just the thing that does that.

DEVELOPING RELATIONSHIPS

Jesus frequently _____ _____ in a discussion of spiritual matters. Because He often made Himself available, He experienced His Father's divine appointments. On day 5 of last week's "My FAITH Journey" (p. 44), we discovered an example from Jesus' life as He approached the woman at the well (see John 4). Jesus had to go through Samaria (see v. 4), a place where He knew He might not be welcome. He established _____ _____ with the woman. He made a transition to _____ _____. He let the woman know how her most pressing need could be met.

When you think about it, witnessing through the relationships we develop in our daily routines is the only way most people will have an opportunity to hear the gospel. Because they are not coming to us, we must go to them. This is the way Jesus communicated. We can follow Jesus' example by starting where lost persons are, by showing that we care about them, and by _____ _____ with them. We can do what Matthew did by _____ _____ to introduce lost persons to Jesus (see Luke 5:27-29). Instead of waiting for lost persons to come to us, we should create opportunities to be with them.

Will McRaney has observed that most Christians live in a world devoid of contact with lost people. He challenges all believers to find ways to have contact with the lost.[1] We cannot dialogue with someone when we don't see him or her. Remember that 80 percent of the unchurched are at least open to attending church with you. The unchurched are waiting and desire to have a relationship with you. We have to wonder what would happen if Christians began to take the initiative rather than waiting for the lost to take the first step. As you develop relationships, FAITH gives you an excellent tool to offer God's gift of salvation to your new friends.

Look at your life-witness summary in last week's "My FAITH Connections" (p. 39). Are you cultivating witnessing relationships with lost persons? ☐ **Yes** ☐ **No**

Have you recently shared the gospel through any of these relationship? ☐ Yes ☐ No

Pray for the lost persons on your life-witness list and for your obedience to share Christ with them.

BECOMING INTENTIONAL IN APPROACH

Taking the initiative to reach lost persons requires being intentional about the ways we view and relate to them. Certain changes can make us more intentional in our approach.

1. Meet physical and emotional _____.
The unchurched will respond more readily to the gospel after they have seen it expressed in ministry.

2. Value the unchurched as _____.
We must value non-Christians as people and seek to develop relationships with them. They are not a project. They are people with the same needs and desires we have.

3. Devote _____ and _____ to reaching the lost.
All of our resources should not be used for the Christians who are already part of the church or class.

4. Seek to understand how non-Christians _____ and _____.
You can read about it, or better yet, you can ask them for yourself. The unchurched are more than willing to tell you what they think and feel if you will simply ask them.

5. Rely on God for _____ in witnessing.
Remember that Christ is by your side and will guide your thoughts and conversations. We must go in His strength and power.

6. Make unbelievers feel that they are _____.
We must be open to the changes in our churches that are needed to make unbelievers feel they are a part even before they accept Christ. We should find it a compliment that unchurched people are turning to us for help.

7. Show _____ by not judging.
We need to accept lost people as they are and not be shocked by the things they may say or do.

8. Make it easy for non-Christians to explore their _____.
Enter dialogue with them about what they and you believe. Drop the church words and tell and show them how your beliefs changed your life.

9. Lead lost persons to a time of _____.
We wouldn't tell someone about a big community event at our church and not invite him or her to attend. That would be rude. Failing to give a non-Christian the

opportunity to respond to Jesus is more than rude; it is cruel. At an appropriate time we must give our non-Christian friends the opportunity to respond.

10. Be a _____ _____.
It's OK for you to talk to lost persons about topics other than spiritual things. That's part of cultivating a relationship. You may even learn something about a hobby, sports, or business.

BECOMING INTENTIONAL IN ACTION

Like Matthew in Jesus' day, we must _____ _____
_____ to introduce lost persons to Jesus in the context of caring relationships. These opportunities should be genuine, authentic times to talk and develop the relationship. Each of the following one-to-one opportunities has been tried with positive results.
1. Fantasy sports leagues (you be the commissioner, and they have to call you every week)
2. Recreational activities (coaching a team or playing on a city recreation team)
3. Exchanging baby-sitting
4. A video of memories (usually done by grandparents who want to share Jesus with their grandchildren)
5. Watching the big game
6. Game nights and dessert, block, and children's parties
7. Moving day (welcome them to the neighborhood)
8. Morning or evening walks
9. Music interests
10. Giving thanks before meals

You are limited only by your creativity as to ways you can connect with the unchurched. You may not see a harvest from every relationship you develop, but you may plant a seed that comes to fruition later. Intentionally establishing and nurturing witnessing relationships should be a regular pattern of life for a Great Commission Christian. Use FAITH to give everyone in your circle of influence the opportunity to experience abundant, eternal life in Jesus Christ.

One way I can connect with unchurched people is ...

_____

_____

_____

One action I need to take to make that happen is ...

_____

_____

_____

Success in any visit occurs not only when a person accepts Christ during a visit but also when teams and individuals are sensitive to new prospects and to the church's potential for future ministry. We cannot control the response a person may give, nor can we force a decision to accept Christ. Our responsibility is to be _____ in going and making disciples. When we are _____ to obey Christ's command, we are successful. John stated that we share "so that our joy may be complete" (1 John 1:4). There is great joy in knowing that you were faithful to God's commands in your life and that you did your part to help others discover Jesus and His forgiveness.

1. Will McRaney Jr., *The Art of Personal Evangelism: Sharing Jesus in a Changing Culture* (Nashville: Broadman and Holman, 2003), 66.

MY FAITH CONNECTIONS

Visitation Summary

Attempts _____
Completed visits _____
Key Question asked _____

Record a synopsis of your team's visits. Include actions you may need to take on needs discovered. Whom should you tell about these needs? Prayer partners? Sunday School teacher? Minister?

_____

_____

_____

_____

Life-Witness Summary

Key Question asked _____

_____

_____

_____

_____

My Journey This Week

What has God taught you this week? Records insights you have gained about God and yourself.

_____

_____

_____

_____

To-Do List

☐ Read session 3
☐ Completed "My FAITH Journey":
  ☐ Day 1
  ☐ Day 2
  ☐ Day 3
  ☐ Day 4
  ☐ Day 5

☐ Secured Sunday School class roll
☐ Contacted prayer partners
☐ Memorized "F Is for *Forgiveness*" section of FAITH presentation
☐ _____
☐ _____
☐ _____
☐ _____
☐ _____
☐ _____

Prayer List

Lost people for whom you are praying:
☐ _____
☐ _____
☐ _____
☐ _____
☐ _____
☐ _____
☐ _____
☐ _____
☐ _____
☐ _____
☐ _____
☐ _____

Others needing prayer:
☐ _____
☐ _____
☐ _____
☐ _____
☐ _____
☐ _____
☐ _____
☐ _____
☐ _____
☐ _____
☐ _____
☐ _____

DAY 1

A young husband is anxiously waiting for his wife to come out of surgery, a delicate surgery to remove a tumor from her face. The doctor finally enters the waiting room and tells the man that all of the tumor was removed, and there will be no need for further treatment. However, the doctor also tells the husband that in order to get all of the tumor, a nerve had to be cut. As a result, the wife's mouth will be twisted on one side of her face. The young husband goes with a nurse to recovery and holds his wife's hand as she recovers from the effects of anesthesia. The doctor enters the recovery room and tells the young bride that all of the tumor was removed. When he explains that the nerve was cut, the young woman asks for a mirror. Looking at her new "smile," she asks the doctor whether her mouth will always be twisted. He nods, wishing he could tell her otherwise. The young husband stands over his wife and begins to admire the new look. All at once he bends down to kiss his wife's crooked mouth, twisting his own lips to accommodate hers.[1]

Think about all the options the young husband faced. What could he have done in that situation?

_____

This husband chose to show his wife that their kiss still worked. Every human is just like that young wife. Because sin has changed us, we are not what we are supposed to be. Our smiles are not right; we too are crooked. And we can do nothing to straighten ourselves out.

Now add God to the scene. Just like the young husband, God could have rejected us. Instead, He saw our need, and Jesus took on our image (see Phil. 2:5-8). He carried the shame of our sin to the cross and died in our place. Just as the young husband demonstrated his love for his bride, Jesus demonstrated His love for us. Jesus was kissing the world, twisting His lips to fit our crooked, needy mouths. He is willing to forgive our sin, accepting us as we are.

The first letter of the FAITH gospel presentation reminds us that we need forgiveness and that Jesus offers it. The outline begins:

F Is for *Forgiveness*
Everyone has sinned and needs God's forgiveness.

"All have sinned and fall short of the glory of God."
Romans 3:23

God's forgiveness is in Jesus only.

"In Him we have redemption through His blood, the forgiveness of our trespasses, according to the riches of His grace."
Ephesians 1:7

Before the next session memorize these statements and Scripture passages. As you do, reflect on God's love for you and His willingness to forgive you.

---

1. Richard Selzer, *Mortal Lessons* (New York: Simon and Schuster, 1974), 45–46.

DAY 2

In the previous session you learned actions to take before and during various kinds of visits. One more action needs to be added to the list, an action that is really personal.

Let's suppose you are an athlete. You have done everything required by the team to prepare for the game. You have practiced hard, memorized all your plays, and studied your opponent's tendencies. As the game approaches, you warm up, stretch, and make sure all your equipment is ready. Once the game starts, you are doing the things asked of you, but you seem a little sluggish. When the coach asks what is wrong, you tell him you are hungry. He asks what you ate for breakfast and lunch, and you tell him you were so busy preparing that you didn't have time to stop for a meal.

How do you think your coach would respond? _____

_____

_____

Most coaches would think you were goofy. The coach would have assumed that you had eaten. Too many times we get so busy preparing to share the gospel that we forget to do one of the main things required of us to succeed—pray.

Esther was a hero in the Old Testament. A plot to extinguish the Hebrew race had been put into action, but Esther intervened and saved her people. After she was challenged to take action, she called for all of the Jews to fast three days for her (see Esth. 4:15-17). She wasn't asking them to pray for her to decide to act; she had already decided she was going to act. She was preparing to act, and she knew God's power would be critical to her success.

We can only imagine what kind of experiences we would have as we visit if every prayer partner and team member fasted in preparation. We are not talking about a show but simply spending time with God in prayer instead of eating lunch or supper prior to visiting.

Consider asking your prayer partners to fast with you when you go out to visit. You can choose a way to fast that is not ostentatious, such as drinking water instead of tea, eating vegetables instead of a meat entrée, or eating a piece of fruit as your meal. The issue is not the details but preparing yourself through prayer.

DAY 3

What if God has placed you in your job so that you can be a missionary? What if God arranged the paths of the people you listed on page 27 so that you could intersect their lives with the truth of the gospel? How do you know He does not have this purpose in mind? What would happen if we began to view every contact we have with another person as having a potential divine purpose?

What feelings do these questions evoke in you? _____

_____

_____

Because God is sovereign, He places His people in strategic places and with purpose. If we really believe that, we will begin to see the people around us as part of God's plan.

Jesus had invited Matthew to follow Him. Leaving everything behind, Matthew began to follow Jesus. Because he was a tax collector, he had numerous contacts with local government officials, businessmen, and other tax collectors. He realized that he knew some people who also needed to meet Jesus, so he decided to throw a big reception for Jesus (see Luke 5:29). The event, which took place at Matthew's house, must have been some party. Even the religious leaders got the word about it (see Luke 5:30). Matthew used his business connections to introduce a large number of people to Jesus.

Matthew could have had a reception for all kinds of reasons, but this reception was intentional. The actions listed in "Becoming Intentional in Action" on page 53 can all be done for a variety of reasons and in some case with no purpose at all. Matthew's reception reminds us that we must be intentional in our actions if we want to help others discover the truth of Jesus for themselves. God gave those contacts to you for a reason.

How can you use the contacts you already have to intentionally introduce others to Jesus?

_____

_____

_____

What actions do you need to take to utilize those contacts for God's glory?

_____

_____

_____

_____

DAY 4

When you look at the two images below, what do you see?

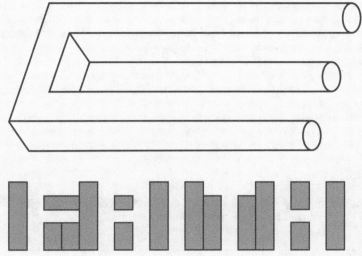

When you look at the images above, you might see one thing, while someone else might see another. Everyone's perspective is different. The same was true for Jesus as He arrived in the city of Bethany three days after the death of his friend Lazarus. To some His coming was the symbol of a missed opportunity (see John 11:21). To others Jesus' arrival was an occasion to question His authority (see John 11:37). For others Jesus' arrival represented another mourner coming to pay his respects (see John 11:35-36). Thomas even saw the arrival as a threat to his own life (see John 11:16).

These perspectives were not what Jesus saw. He saw an opportunity to bring glory to God and to demonstrate why people could believe in Him (see John 11:4,42). They were all looking at the same cave. Most saw a hopeless situation. Jesus saw an opportunity.

When you look at the names of the persons on your Sunday School class roll, what do you see? If your class is like most, some people never attend, and some seem to be hopeless cases. Maybe you would like to remove some from the roll. The reality is that each person on that roll represents an opportunity. They are more than names. They are real people with real needs and desires. Until they move or tell you never to contact them again, they remain your class's responsibility. You must believe that you have their names for a reason. Your class must ask itself, *What do we see when we read the names of the persons on that roll?*

Review the roll for the Sunday School class you attend. You may need to contact your Sunday School teacher or another class leader to get that information. Look at the names and begin to pray for them. Ask God to show you the opportunities He may be placing before you.

DAY 5

The following is an excerpt from a journal:

Yesterday I shared Christ with my granddad. It was the first time I had seen him in five years. He is not well. Dad asked me to go see him, so I did. All the way I rehearsed my conversation, hoping we would get to talk about spiritual things. Once I was there, he asked the question I had been praying he would ask, and I did just what I had rehearsed. I knew how it was supposed to end, but it didn't end that way. All he told me was that he was scared of dying and wanted me to pray. He wouldn't let me go beyond that. What I thought was going to be one of those special stories turned into a frustrating experience. Eventually, I prayed for him just as he had asked, and Dad and I left.

Today when driving back, I relived the conversation, trying to see where I had failed. In the middle of my drive, two realities hit me. For the first time my dad had seen me trying to lead another person to Christ. The second reality was that if my granddad ended up in hell, it wouldn't be because of me. I had told him what he needed to do. I pray that he makes the decision before he dies.

Review the definition of success on page 54. Would you consider the situation described in the journal to be a success? Why or why not?

_____

_____

_____

_____

When writing to the Corinthian church, Paul declared that he had "become all things to all people, so that I may by all means save some" (1 Cor. 9:22). He did not expect everyone he encountered to accept the message he was delivering. Not everyone who listened to Jesus' sermons received Him either.

Too many times we feel that the only type of success in witnessing is having a person accept Christ. While that is certainly hoped for, success is found in being faithful regardless of the results. We are responsible only for that which we can control. We cannot control the way a person responds to the gospel. However, we can control whether the gospel was shared and whether the person was given an opportunity to respond.

Another entry in the same journal four years later reads:

Today we buried Granddad. A minister who once lived across the street from him told us about leading my granddad to Jesus. We didn't know for sure until today. I may never know why Granddad didn't tell me about this on that day I went to see him. That doesn't matter today. All I know is that Granddad accepted Christ at some time in his life, and I look forward to seeing him in heaven someday.

Take time to thank God for the opportunity to share with others. Thank Him for others who are seeking to share Jesus as well. Ask Him to help you be faithful regardless of the results.

SESSION

F IS FOR *FORGIVENESS*

SESSION GOALS

You will—
- describe the nature of lostness and sin;
- gain an understanding that F is for *forgiveness*;
- identify why people need forgiveness;
- explain why forgiveness is through Jesus only;
- identify key points about forgiveness that may require specific attention.

Everyone has sinned and needs God's forgiveness.

"All have sinned and fall short of the glory of God."
Romans 3:23

God's forgiveness is in Jesus only.

*"In Him we have redemption through His blood, the forgiveness
of our trespasses, according to the riches of His grace."*
Ephesians 1:7

*Think about a time when you got lost on your way somewhere. What destination
were you seeking?*

_____

Where were you when you realized you were lost? _____

_____

How did you finally get to the right destination? _____

_____

_____

Luke 15 records Jesus' parables of the lost sheep, the lost coin, and the lost (or prodigal) son. The idea of being lost is commonly used to describe a person who has not accepted Jesus as Savior and Lord. To be lost means to be out of place. Lostness describes someone's _____ more than his or her destination. We are lost before we arrive at the wrong destination.

All humanity was created to be in _____ with God. We are supposed to be with Him. When we are separated from God, we are not where we are supposed to be; thus, we are lost. We are separated from God by _____. A by-product of our sin is being lost and therefore not with Him. Because of this sin we need forgiveness so that we can be where we are supposed to be: in a personal relationship with God.

Each letter in the FAITH gospel presentation uses one or more verses of Scripture to explain the significance of that letter. The verse(s) are used in the presentation to help you confirm what God says in the Bible.

Many wonderful verses in God's Word highlight forgiveness. New Testament Scriptures that highlight forgiveness include Matthew 6:14; 26:28; Mark 1:4; 2:5; Acts 5:31; 8:22; Romans 3:25; 4:7. The Greek word for *forgiveness* used in these passages means *to let go, to leave, to leave behind,* and *to remit.* The idea conveyed is that something has been let go, never to be returned to for future reference.

Forgiveness is more than reconciliation—two parties being brought back together. It also involves completely forgetting the offense that initially caused the problem. The Bible tells us that when God forgives us, He _____ our sin, never to bring it up again (see Jer. 31:34).

The New Testament depicts forgiveness as coming from God, constantly needed, granted when requested, and based on the _____ _____ of _____. It also indicates future blessing. Related concepts make it plain that forgiveness is God's responsibility as Judge, has its basis in His saving act in Christ, begins the process of transformation toward godly character, brings total renewal in the future, and is received when God's judgment is affirmed in the confession of sin.

When a person is lost, four possible things could be going on:
1. He could not know he is lost.
2. He could know he is lost but refuse to admit it.
3. He could try to find the way to God on his own.
4. He could admit he is lost and get the help he needs.

As believers, we have a responsibility to help others realize they are lost, admit it, humbly acknowledge that they cannot find their way on their own, and introduce them to the One who can help them.

F IS FOR *FORGIVENESS*

Each letter in the word *FAITH* relates to a word that helps you explain how to know Jesus as Savior. Each word is easy to remember. By using the word *forgiveness* for the letter F, you have the opportunity to remind people of their _____ for forgiveness and to establish the fact that only _____ can provide it. The letter F stands for *forgiveness*.

Everyone has sinned and needs God's forgiveness.

"All have sinned and fall short of the glory of God."
Romans 3:23

God's forgiveness is in Jesus only.

"In Him we have redemption through His blood, the forgiveness of our trespasses, according to the riches of His grace."
Ephesians 1:7

Think back to the time when you were lost, which you identified earlier.

What emotions did you feel when you were lost? _____

_____

_____

_____

What factors caused you to believe you were going the right direction when in reality you were going the wrong way?

_____

_____

_____

_____

While you were lost, did you remain confident that you were going in the right direction? ☐ Yes ☐ No

Remembering the time you were lost and focusing on the way you felt can help you relate to and help people who are spiritually lost.

Review the first point in your evangelistic story, which you recorded on page 26 in "My FAITH Journey." How did you realize you were lost?

_____

_____

_____

_____

_____

How long did you continue your search after you realized you were lost?

_____

Think about a friend or an acquaintance you know is lost, perhaps one of the people you are praying for or with whom you are cultivating a friendship. How would you rank this person's awareness of his or her lostness on the following scale? Write the person's name above the appropriate number.

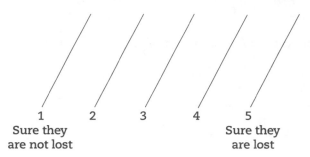

1	2	3	4	5
Sure they are not lost				Sure they are lost

EVERYONE HAS SINNED AND NEEDS GOD'S FORGIVENESS

What do you think causes non-Christians to move from being sure they are not spiritually lost to being less sure about their spiritual condition and being willing to admit that they may be lost? It begins with an understanding of sin. The Bible puts it this way: "All have sinned and fall short of the glory of God" (Rom. 3:23).

This verse highlights the fact that everyone is a sinner and needs God's forgiveness. Our need for forgiveness is set against the backdrop of _____. His life exemplified _____ and _____ in every way. It is by Jesus' sinless life that all humans are to be judged as being worthy or unworthy of entrance into heaven. No one can obtain that standard and is therefore already a _____ person. This judgment also comes as a result of someone's _____—the rejection of God's revelation in Jesus Christ (see John 3:18-19; 16:8-16).

Sin results in broken _____ with God. The ideal life is one of fellowship with God. Anything that disturbs, distorts, or breaks this fellowship is _____. Jesus forcefully taught that sin is more a condition of the _____ than a specific, visible action. He traced sin directly to inner motives, stating that a sinful thought leading to an overt act is the real sin. Anger in the heart is sin, just as murder is sin (see Matt. 5:21-22). An impure look is sin, just as adultery is sin (see Matt. 5:27-28). The real defilement in a person stems from the inner person (heart), which is sinful (see Matt. 15:18-20). Sin, therefore, involves a person's essential being, that is, the essence of human nature.

Sin is also revealed by the law of Moses. The law revealed sin in its true character. The law as such is not bad, but humanity simply does not have the ability to keep the law. Therefore, the law offers no means of salvation; rather, it leaves humanity with a deep sense of sin and guilt (see Rom. 7). The law serves as a means to demonstrate our need, pointing us to Jesus and His forgiveness. That means _____ [insert your name] has sinned and has fallen short of God's glory.

GOD'S FORGIVENESS IS IN JESUS ONLY

"In Him we have redemption through His blood, the forgiveness of our trespasses, according to the riches of His grace."
Ephesians 1:7

Ephesians 1:7 highlights the fact that God's forgiveness is found in _____ _____. We can do a lot of things to try and deal with our sin. We can even make ourselves look fairly good and upright but still be out of place—lost. As long as we are without Jesus, we are lost. The good news is that forgiveness can be found in Jesus. We will discover more about this truth when we examine John 14:6 in session 7, *"T Is for Turn."*

Forgiveness is not based on what we have _____, how _____ we are, or how _____ we are. A lot of people are sincere about their beliefs. Jesus made it clear to the religious leaders of His day that although they were sincere in their practice, they were also sincerely wrong. Calling them hypocrites and blind guides, He denounced their diligence in their religious duties because they "neglected the more important matters of the law—justice, mercy, and faith" (Matt. 23:23).

Our culture encourages us to accept other beliefs, regardless of biblical absolutes or moral standards. Tolerance is one of the biggest weapons of deception that Satan uses in our world. If a person dies holding a belief in anyone or anything other than Jesus, he will be sincerely and eternally regretful. Lost is lost, no matter how sincere.

Forgiveness is based on the _____ that Jesus Christ made for our sins when He died on the cross. It is by His death and His death alone that we can be forgiven. We can experience the joy of forgiveness in no other way.

God created the universe, and that includes all humanity. We were created for fellowship with Him. Sin broke that fellowship, separating us from God and making it impossible for us to be what God created us to be. The price of sin is _____: "The wages of sin is death, but the gift of God is eternal life in Christ Jesus our Lord" (Rom. 6:23). Death is the wage to be paid for sin. That is the fee, and that price is not negotiable. Instead of giving up on His creation, God made it possible for sinful people to fulfill their purpose of having a relationship with Him. For that relationship to be restored, the price for sin had to be paid. The sacrifice would need to be perfect, without sin. Only a perfect person would be qualified to pay the price of sin for others.

Jesus left heaven and lived a perfect, sinless life as a human. By being fully human and fully divine, Jesus met the requirement of being a _____ _____. Ephesians 1:7 states that the shedding of Jesus' _____ accomplished our redemption. *To redeem* means "to secure the release of something or someone. It connotes the idea of paying what is required in order to liberate from oppression, enslavement, or another type of binding obligation."[1] Jesus' crucifixion paid the price for our sin. Neither Muhammad, Buddha, Confucius, nor any other religious figure qualified to pay the price for our sin. Only Jesus could and did pay that price. That is why He and He alone is the source of forgiveness from sin.

Ephesians 1:7 also reminds us that God's forgiveness is an act of _____. *Grace is the undeserved acceptance and love received from another, especially the characteristic attitude of God in providing salvation for sinners.* For Christians the word *grace* is virtually synonymous with the gospel of God's gift of unmerited salvation in Jesus Christ. To express this idea, the New Testament writers used the Greek word *charis*, which had a long previous history in secular Greek. Related to the word for *joy* or *pleasure*, *charis* originally referred to something delightful or attractive in a person, something that brought pleasure to others.

Paul's understanding of God's grace came from his life experiences. He had been turned from the persecutor of the church to Christ's missionary to the Gentiles (see 1 Cor. 15:9-10; 1 Tim. 1:12-14). As a Pharisee Paul had sought to live by the divine law. Now he knew that salvation was not a matter of earning God's acceptance but rather accepting God's acceptance of him through Jesus Christ. So the apostle saw a sharp difference between law and grace. Law is the way of self-help, of earning one's own way. Grace is God's way of salvation, totally unearned. It is open to all people but is conditioned on their response. People are free to accept or reject it.

How would you summarize God's grace in one sentence? _____

_____

_____

_____

OPPORTUNITIES FOR CONTINUED DIALOGUE

As you discuss F is for *forgiveness* in the FAITH gospel presentation, the lost person may respond to what you have said by asking questions like these.

1. Wasn't there _____ _____?

As we discovered in session 2, many lost people will respond to the Key Question with a works answer (see pp. 35–36), thinking they can earn or make their own way to God. The problem is that there is no other way. The Bible is clear about this. When people question that Jesus is the source of forgiveness, ask them what they believe about Him. If they believe Jesus was a great teacher, explain that for a person to be a great teacher, he or she must teach the truth. Ask whether they have ever studied Jesus' teachings. Using the verses included in the FAITH gospel presentation that quote Jesus Himself, highlight Jesus' teachings that He is the only way to heaven. For example, John 14:6 quotes Jesus as saying, "I am the way, the truth, and the life. No one comes to the Father except through Me."

2. Why do I need _____?

If, during the presentation of the gospel, someone protests that he or she hasn't been that bad, you may need to deal with that assertion now. A person really can't understand the rest of the presentation if he or she doesn't believe he or she is a sinner who needs forgiveness.

Begin by explaining that sin can be placed in one of three categories:

1. Sins of _____: actions you commit against another, including God
2. Sins of _____: good things you fail to do
3. _____ sins: attitudes against another person or against God

Most people understand sin in terms of commission, ignoring the sins of omission and secrecy. Others would admit to some type of sin in these areas. The lost person needs to understand that from God's perspective, all of these are sins that make the person guilty.

Also address the mistake of categorizing sin into various levels of severity. A person may argue that he has not murdered anyone or is a law-abiding citizen. Without question certain sins carry greater consequences than others. Premeditated murder carries a greater consequence than writing bad checks. Our legal system is built on the concept of greater consequence. However, to the one who received the bad check, it really didn't matter if the person writing the check wasn't guilty of a greater crime. The Bible doesn't categorize some sins as more or less serious than others. Sin is sin, regardless of our assessment of its severity (see Jas. 2:8-11). Therefore, everyone is a sinner and needs God's forgiveness.

GETTING PERSONAL

Consider what the truth of God's forgiveness means for you as someone who has been saved by His grace. First, as a believer you can quit beating yourself up for your _____. We all have a past and have done things of which we are ashamed. Moses killed a man; yet God still used him to lead the Hebrews out of Egypt. Psalm 103:10-12 reminds us:

> He has not dealt with us as our sins deserve
> or repaid us according to our offenses.
> For as high as the heavens are above the earth,
> so great is His faithful love
> toward those who fear Him.
> As far as the east is from the west,
> so far has He removed
> our transgressions from us.

Because you have been saved, you don't have to live under the cloud of your past.

Do you need to take any action to reconcile a broken relationship or to make restitution to someone for a sin you committed in the past? ☐ Yes ☐ No

We also have a responsibility to follow the _____ of our Heavenly Father: if God is in the business of forgiving, then so are His _____ (see Mark 11:25). If we are to exhibit His character in our lives, we must ask God to help us learn to forgive others.

Do you need to forgive someone?   ☐ **Yes**   ☐ **No**

We must not keep others from being all God wants them to be because we are unwilling to forgive them. Bitterness and an unforgiving spirit poison the heart over time. Just as God has forgiven us, we must be willing to forgive others.

1. Stan Norman, *Holman Illustrated Bible Dictionary* (Nashville: Holman Bible Publishers, 2003), 1370.

MY FAITH CONNECTIONS

Visitation Summary

Attempts _____
Completed visits _____
Key Question asked _____

Record a synopsis of your team's visits. Include actions you may need to take on needs discovered. Whom should you tell about these needs? Prayer partners? Sunday School teacher? Minister?

_____
_____
_____
_____
_____

Life-Witness Summary

Key Question asked _____

_____
_____
_____
_____

My Journey This Week

What has God taught you this week? Records insights you have gained about God and yourself.

_____
_____
_____
_____

To-Do List

☐ Read session 4
☐ Completed "My FAITH Journey":
　☐ Day 1
　☐ Day 2
　☐ Day 3
　☐ Day 4
　☐ Day 5

☐ Asked a friend or family member the Key Question
☐ Contacted prayer partners
☐ Memorized "A Is for *Available*" section of FAITH presentation
☐ Reviewed "F Is for *Forgiveness*" section of FAITH presentation
☐ _____
☐ _____
☐ _____
☐ _____
☐ _____
☐ _____

Prayer List

Lost people for whom you are praying:
☐ _____
☐ _____
☐ _____
☐ _____
☐ _____
☐ _____
☐ _____
☐ _____
☐ _____
☐ _____

Others needing prayer:
☐ _____
☐ _____
☐ _____
☐ _____
☐ _____
☐ _____
☐ _____
☐ _____
☐ _____
☐ _____

DAY 1

This week you studied F is for *forgiveness* in the FAITH gospel presentation. The next session will focus on A is for *available*. Today let's look ahead and start getting ready for the next step in the outline.

Imagine you are dune buggying in a desert and have lost your way. All you see for miles is sand. It is high noon, so you can't even use the sun to help you guess which direction is east or west. Even though you don't know which way to go, you decide to set out, hoping to find something by driving. Eventually, you top a sand dune and see a convenience store sitting on a two-lane road. How would you respond on first seeing that store?

Most of us would be relieved and happy. The store represents the possibility of no longer being lost. Someone in the store could help you find your way or at least sell you a map that would help you know which way to go. For the person who is spiritually lost, the truth of the gospel represents the possibility of no longer being lost and, in addition, being saved and restored.

With the letter F we discovered that everyone needs forgiveness and that it can be found in Jesus. The good news is that God's forgiveness is available. The availability of forgiveness is what the second letter in the word *FAITH* addresses.

The person who was lost in the desert found help when he located the store. More importantly, the person who is lost in sin will find the way out by coming to know Jesus. In John 3:16 Jesus said, "God loved the world in this way: He gave His One and Only Son, so that everyone who believes in Him will not perish but have eternal life." Underline the word *everyone* to remind yourself that no one is left out. It is possible for anyone to be forgiven by God, regardless of what he or she has done in the past.

Here is the other side of God's forgiveness being available: it is not automatic. Suppose the person in the dune buggy simply stopped and admired the store he discovered. Or suppose he ignored the store and passed by, going straight to the paved road in the assumption it would get him somewhere. In both cases he would still be lost, not knowing where he was supposed to be.

Jesus stated, "Not everyone who says to Me, 'Lord, Lord!' will enter the kingdom of heaven" (Matt 7:21). God's forgiveness is not automatic. An action is required for someone to have God's forgiveness.

In session 5 we will more fully examine A is for *available*. Begin to memorize the Scripture verses included with this section of the FAITH gospel presentation while continuing to review F is for *forgiveness*.

DAY 2

Think of all the excuses a person can use for sinful actions:
- It's a disease.
- I was born this way.
- I'm only human.
- It wasn't as bad as it could have been.
- It all ended up OK.
- I had no other choice; you wouldn't want me to hurt someone's feelings, would you?
- No one was hurt.

These are just a few excuses we may have heard when it comes to sin. If we tried, we could add even more to the list. If we were honest, we would admit we have made excuses for our sinful actions. Many of us would even have to admit that we have found a way to justify some of those actions. Unfortunately, we can justify almost anything if we really try.

Our culture is increasingly desensitized to sin. We see it on television, at the movies, and in advertising. We do all kinds of things to make it sound less offensive. Terms like *prochoice* and *alternative lifestyle* point to our society's efforts to minimize the seriousness of sin.

The truth is that sin is not pretty. It separates us from God and keeps us from being what God created us to be. Although issues like war, famine, and global warming are important, calling for prayer and a Christian response, sin is the number one problem in our world. The fact that Jesus left heaven to address sin demonstrates how big a problem it is.

Meditate on Romans 3:23, focusing on each phrase. Record your thoughts as you reflect on each section. What other Bible verses come to mind as you consider the truth of this passage?

All: _____

_____

Have sinned: _____

_____

_____

And fall short: _____

_____

_____

Of the glory of God: _____

_____

DAY 3

We all have people in our lives whom we love.

List the five persons you love most in the world.

1. _____   4. _____
2. _____   5. _____
3. _____

Circle one of the names. How could you demonstrate your love for that person in such a way that he or she would have no doubt of your love?

_____

_____

Hopefully, you thought of all kinds of ways you could demonstrate love for the person you identified. Some of the things you considered could have been simple and inexpensive, while other actions could have carried great price tags. For example, you may know a person who has donated a kidney to a family member or a friend. Without that person's sacrifice the other person would have died. That may be an extreme example, but Jesus took it one step further. He declared that the greatest way a person could demonstrate love to another would be to die so that the other person could live (see John 15:13). That was Jesus' mission.

In Ephesians 1:7 Paul declared that we are redeemed through Jesus' blood. Paul understood that Jesus demonstrated His love for humanity through His death (see Rom. 5:8). Jesus' sacrifice was truly an act of love.

Read Isaiah 53 and list the actions the prophet said the servant would carry out.

_____

_____

Several of these prophetic verses were linked to Jesus (see Matt. 8:17; 26:64; 27:46; Luke 22:37; Acts 8:32-33; Heb. 9:28). There is no doubt that the servant in Isaiah 53 was Jesus.

List ways Jesus has demonstrated His love for you. _____

_____

_____

_____

Jesus expressed His love for you through sacrifice and service. Stop and thank Jesus for loving you and for securing your forgiveness by His death. As you go through the day, seek to demonstrate love and sacrificial service to one of the persons you identified.

MY FAITH JOURNEY

DAY 4

Deborah was excited about visiting most people. She enjoyed getting to know people and was very comfortable talking about spiritual things. However, she continued to avoid one assignment. A name had been given to her FAITH team, and it seemed that they were never able to go by and visit that person. Deborah even suggested one night that they do Opinion Polls instead of "going all the way to the other side of town."

Noticing that the visit had not been made, the FAITH coordinator asked about the assigned person. Deborah admitted that she and the person assigned to her team had attended high school together, where Deborah had been a cheerleader. Deborah confessed that she had sabotaged the other person's campaign to become a cheerleader. Twenty years had passed since Deborah had graduated from high school, and she needed to ask for forgiveness.

She is not alone in needing to get some things right from the past. Sometimes the failure to reconcile past wrongs keeps us from effectively representing Christ in the world. Reread "Getting Personal" on pages 67–68.

When seeking forgiveness from someone, Ken Sande suggests using these principles:
- Address everyone involved.
- Avoid *if*, *but*, and *maybe*.
- Admit specifically what you did.
- Acknowledge the hurt.
- Accept the consequences.
- Alter your behavior, telling others what you are doing now.
- Ask for forgiveness.
- Allow time.[1]

Above all, we need to tell God and the person we offended that we are sorry.

Have you committed an offense for which you need to ask forgiveness?
❏ Yes   ❏ No

If so, first pause to pray, agreeing with God about this sin and asking for His forgiveness.

Now write the things you need to do to correct the past wrong. Begin putting specific steps into action to ask forgiveness and seek reconciliation.

_____

_____

_____

_____

_____

1. Ken Sande, *The Peacemaker* (Grand Rapids, MI: Baker Books, 2004), 127–33.

DAY 5

Dr. Thom Rainer led a team of researchers who conducted surveys of lost people across the United States. They went to malls, bookstores, coffeehouses, and hangouts of all kinds to conduct these interviews. They were very careful to gather information from people who were not followers of Jesus. The information was then compiled and organized. The result was a book titled The Unchurched Next Door. *The researchers identified five major groups or categories of lost people in the United States. On day 5 of the next five weeks, we will examine one of the five categories and characteristics of lost people in that category.*

Michelle is an example of the first category, U1, or highly receptive. She attended VBS as a child, but that's the extent of her spiritual training. Because she is married and has a child, Sunday is the only day for the family to rest and relax. When Michelle was interviewed, she was extremely friendly and receptive to the idea of church and God. Even though she is illiterate in regard to the Bible, she is interested in learning what it says. At the end of the interview, Michelle indicated that she and her husband had discussed attending a church. The interviewer noted, "Although she was running short on time, she allowed me to tell her briefly the plan of salvation. I know she was interested in talking more about heaven and hell, and I think she will soon go to church with a friend so that her child can be in church."[1]

Michelle is typical of the highly receptive in the following ways.
- She is interested in Bible study.
- She has some, though minimal, church experiences.
- She has a favorable view of the church and ministers.
- She has some ideas about spiritual things.
- She is concerned about her family.

What distinguishes people in this group from others is that not only are they willing to dialogue about spiritual things, but they may also initiate dialogue.

This group represents 11 percent of the lost in the United States[2]—nearly 17 million people. This means that statistically, 1 in every 10 lost persons we encounter will be highly receptive. That is encouraging to know, especially when we conduct Opinion Polls.

As you consider the characteristics of the highly receptive, look at the list of persons you are seeking to reach (see "My FAITH Connections," p. 69). Whom would you describe as highly receptive?

_____

What immediate actions do you need to take? _____

_____

_____

1. Thom S. Rainer, *The Unchurched Next Door* (Grand Rapids, MI: Zondervan, 2003), 183.
2. Ibid., 261.

SESSION

A IS FOR *AVAILABLE*

SESSION GOALS

You will—
- identify the alls of the Great Commission;
- discover that God's forgiveness is available for all;
- understand why God's forgiveness is not automatic;
- identify ways your belief that Jesus is the only way affects you, your Sunday School or small group, and your church;
- examine biblical evidence that Christianity is both inclusive and exclusive.

God's forgiveness is available for all.

"God loved the world in this way: He gave His One and Only Son, so that everyone who believes in Him will not perish but have eternal life."
John 3:16

God's forgiveness is available but not automatic.

"Not everyone who says to Me, 'Lord, Lord!' will enter the kingdom of heaven."
Matthew 7:21

If you found out your favorite aunt or uncle had bought a gift for you and wanted you to come pick it up, would you do it? Most of us would be on our way as soon as we could. When we arrived, we would start looking for that gift and asking whether we could open it.

We can think of God's forgiveness as a gift waiting to be opened. During this session we will discover that the second letter in the word FAITH stands for *available*. God's gift of forgiveness is available.

THE ALLS OF THE GREAT COMMISSION

Although several passages in the New Testament instruct believers to share Jesus with others, Matthew 28:18-20 is probably the most familiar. Although we examined those verses in session 1, we need to examine one more element of Jesus' commission.

Read Jesus' Great Commission and circle all uses of the word all or similar words.

> "All authority has been given to Me in heaven and on earth. Go, therefore, and make disciples of all nations, baptizing them in the name of the Father and of the Son and of the Holy Spirit, teaching them to observe everything I have commanded you. And remember, I am with you always, to the end of the age." Matthew 28:18-20

Jesus began by saying that *all* _____ or power is given to Him. Jesus has the authority to tell us what to do! Christ told us to go and make disciples of *all* _____. We are to teach people to do *all* _____ Christ commanded us to do. And remember, He is with us *always*—at *all* _____ and in *all* _____.

Jesus had a reason for using the word *all* so much. His commission to us is for all times and places. Our responsibility is greater than participating in FAITH visitation. It includes being a witness at work, while playing sports, and even when things don't go our way. The practice of being a disciple and making disciples is a _____ and an _____, not an event or a once-a-week activity. It is also a lifestyle and an attitude for which Jesus provides His power and presence.

GOOD NEWS: GOD'S FORGIVENESS IS AVAILABLE FOR ALL!

In response to someone's answer to the Key Question and willingness to know what the Bible says, you have already shared that we cannot have eternal life and heaven without God's forgiveness. Now you have the opportunity to share good news about the availability of God's forgiveness. The letter A in FAITH stands for *available*.

God's forgiveness is available for all.

"God loved the world in this way: He gave His One and Only Son, so that everyone who believes in Him will not perish but have eternal life."
John 3:16

John 3:16 highlights God's forgiveness—for ourselves and for all people. It is so personal. Gifts are always personal. The best gifts are the ones that fit the person receiving the gift or that fill a need in his or her life. To give the perfect gift, the giver has to know exactly what the potential receiver likes or needs. _____ was the perfect gift.

All humans were created to have _____ with God. That relationship makes us thrive. Being in relationship with Him is what we like and need. However, our _____ wouldn't allow us to have a relationship with God, so the gift of Jesus met our need for _____. God, the perfect gift giver, gave us the perfect gift, His Son, so that we could live a life in relationship with Him, a life filled with purpose, meaning, and hope.

Write your name in each blank in the following paraphrase as you recall the personal nature of God's love.

God loved _____ *in this way: He gave His One and Only Son, so that when* _____ *believes in Him,* _____ *will not perish but have eternal life.*

GOD'S FORGIVENESS IS NOT AUTOMATIC

God's forgiveness is available but not automatic.

"Not everyone who says to Me, 'Lord, Lord!' will enter the kingdom of heaven."
Matthew 7:21

It is much easier to understand that God's forgiveness is _____ for all than to recognize that His forgiveness is not _____. What does it mean to you that God's forgiveness is not automatic?

God wants all people to accept His forgiveness. That's why sharing with everyone we possibly can is so important, even though some will reject the good news.

Many verses in Scripture remind us that God wants all people to _____ His forgiveness. Many of those same verses also indicate that not everyone will _____ to accept it. Matthew 7:13-14 underscores this reality: "The gate is wide and the road is broad that leads to destruction, and there are many who go through it. How narrow is the gate and difficult the road that leads to life, and few find it." Jesus made this statement while preaching one of the most famous sermons in history, the Sermon on the Mount (Matt. 5–7). In that same sermon Jesus declared, "Not everyone who says to Me, 'Lord, Lord!' will enter the kingdom of heaven, but only the one who does the will of My Father in heaven. On that day many will say to Me, 'Lord, Lord, didn't we prophesy in Your name, drive out demons in Your name, and do many miracles in Your name?' Then I will announce to them, 'I never knew you! Depart from Me, you lawbreakers!' " (Matt. 7:21-24).

Many of the people who heard this sermon were religious, some even religious leaders of their day. Jesus' words remind us that it is not about _____ or keeping a set of _____. It is about an intimate _____ _____ with Him. Religion can ease our guilt, but it will never give us entrance into heaven.

REGAINING OUR FOCUS ON THE LOST

The fact that God's forgiveness is not automatic reminds us of the great cost of this gift: the death of His Son, Jesus. And not everyone will choose to accept His great gift. If we ever really understand that people are not automatically granted salvation apart from accepting Jesus, we will sense a greater _____ in being a witness.

Do you truly believe that the only way to God is through Jesus? □ Yes □ No
How does your life demonstrate this belief?

_____

_____

Evaluate your church in focusing on the lost. Check the actions that characterize your church.
□ *Go to the lost rather than expect the lost to come to you.*
□ *Meet physical and emotional needs as well as spiritual needs of lost people.*
□ *Value non-Christians as people and seek to develop relationships.*
□ *Encourage church and Sunday School leaders to devote time and resources to reach the lost rather than to focus primarily on Christians who are already part of the church.*
□ *Join with other Christians to learn more about lost people.*
□ *Make it easy for non-Christians to explore their beliefs in your church.*
□ *Make sure new people feel welcome.*
□ *Lovingly challenge your non-Christian friends to commit their lives to Christ.*[1]

These actions also define a person who understands that forgiveness is not automatic. How well did these things describe you? On a scale of 1 to 10, how would you rate your concern for others' salvation?

1	2	3	4	5	6	7	8	9	10
Couldn't care less							Very concerned		

OPPORTUNITIES FOR CONTINUED DIALOGUE

When you present *A is for available* as part of the FAITH gospel presentation, the lost person may ask questions like the following.

1. Won't _____ be saved?

When examining John 3:16, some people are blinded by the word *all* ("everyone") and do not see "everyone who believes in Him [meaning Jesus]" as being the absolute requirement for salvation. The idea that everyone will eventually gain heaven is called _____. The phrase "All religions lead to God" characterizes this belief. Universalism is considered inclusive: as long as a person's beliefs are sincere, he or she will be saved.

One challenge to the sharing the gospel in our society today is tolerance. Those who promote tolerance oppose the gospel of Jesus because they feel it is intolerant and inherently critical of others' beliefs. Of course, every Christian believes in religious freedom, but a tragic danger lies in thoughtless tolerance that denies a Christian's right to tell the truth of salvation in Jesus Christ. The intolerant promoters of tolerance are quickly turning our society and civilization into an ungodly wilderness wasteland. There is a difference between recognizing a person's right to decide and redefining every religion as one of many ways to God. Regardless of how a person feels about tolerance, the fact remains that someone is wrong. We all can't be right!

We must help people understand that in reality Christianity is _____; God offered the opportunity for forgiveness for all when Jesus said "everyone" in John 3:16. Even so, Christianity is _____ in that Jesus Christ is the only way to the Father and heaven (see John 14:6). Just as we don't possess a gift until we receive it by taking it from the giver, we don't possess God's gift of forgiveness until we receive it.

This may be the most misunderstood point in the gospel. Many people seem to believe that entering heaven when we die is more or less automatic. Paul stated, "The god of this age has blinded the minds of the unbelievers so they cannot see the light of the gospel of the glory of Christ, who is the image of God" (2 Cor. 4:4). The more you engage in dialogue with others about Jesus, the more you will realize the truth of this verse. Most people seem to think they are acceptable to God because they judge themselves horizontally—in comparison to their neighbors, feeling they are as good as the person next door. The reality and problem are that we are judged vertically—by the absolute requirements of the holy God.

2. How can a loving God send someone to _____?

When sharing that forgiveness is not automatic, some will object to the idea of God's sending people to a place like hell. Some may even question the existence of hell. At the core of this issue is a faulty understanding of _____. When dialoguing with a person who questions how a loving God could send a person to hell, begin by asking the person to define God. Remember that each of the many different religious systems in our world has a different understanding of God. After the person has described his or her idea, ask whether you can share what the Bible says about God.

The God of the Bible is the personal _____ who is "worthy of human _____ because of His holy _____ and His perfect _____, revealed in creating the universe, electing and redeeming His people, and providing eternal salvation through His Son Jesus Christ."[2] The Bible defines God by giving His characteristics. Here is a partial list of those characteristics.

- God is the only true God (see Jer. 10:10).
- God is the living God (see Isa. 41:22-24; 44:9-20; 46:1-2,6-7).
- God is Lord and Master (see Ex. 34:24).
- God is holy (see Isa. 5:16; 6:3; 1 Pet. 1:15-16).
- God is eternal (see Rev. 22:13).
- God is spirit (see Gen. 1:3).
- God is love (see 1 John 4:8,16).
- God is Father (see Matt. 5:43-48; Luke 11:2, 13; Gal. 3:26).
- God is intimate and personal (see Ex. 34:14; Nah. 1:2; 1 Cor. 10:22).
- God is glorious (see Ex. 16:7-10; Isa. 6:3; Eph. 1:12-17; Heb. 1:3).
- God is wise (see Job 11:4-12; 28:1-28; Ps. 139; Rom. 11).
- God is all-powerful (see Isa. 40:10-31; 1 Cor. 1:18-25).
- God is righteous (see Ex. 2:23-25).[3]

All the character traits of God work together in perfect _____. He is love (see 1 John 4:8,16), but He is more than love. If God did not punish sin, He would in effect violate His own nature and would therefore be out of balance. Being out of balance would then disqualify Him from being God. That will not happen. The question about God's sending a person to hell is really the wrong question. The real question is, How can a perfect God have a relationship with someone who is _____ and _____?

Jesus addressed this issue when talking with Nicodemus. In the verses following John 3:16, Jesus told Nicodemus that "anyone who believes in Him is not condemned, but anyone who does not believe is already condemned" (John 3:18). Jesus did not say He would send people to hell. They were already on their way due to their own decisions and sin. Jesus didn't come to _____ people to hell. He came to _____ them from hell.

The lost person may also be asking how a loving God can choose not to act so that at least some of those He loves can be saved. God's desire is for _____ _____ to be saved (see 2 Pet. 3:9). Seeing His creation reject Him and choose its own way over Him does not bring God joy, but His perfect righteousness and holiness demand judgment for sin. It is by our own doing, not His, that some will spend eternity in hell.

GETTING PERSONAL

John 3:16 reminds us that the gospel is for _____. Do you really believe that? What does it mean to *you* that forgiveness is available for all? Unless you understand and believe that God's love is available for each person, including each person with whom you come in contact, you have missed the full impact of God's _____.

Although we may be reluctant to admit it, most of us could probably identify a person, a group, or a class of people we would rather not see in heaven. Realize that God's forgiveness is available to them just as it is available to you. God is willing and able to rescue anyone.

Are you willing to ask God to help you overcome any biases you may have toward people so that you will be willing to reach everyone with the gospel? □ Yes □ No

Do you need to pray that a particular person will accept God's offer of forgiveness? □ Yes □ No

"Not automatic" means that some will not make it to heaven. This reality should break our hearts. Some of these are our neighbors, friends, and relatives; the list could go on. They will spend eternity in hell. When we are sitting at a red light, do we regard the people in the cars around us as perhaps being on the road to hell? What about the people we come in contact with every week—waiters, gas-station attendants, sales clerks, and department-store greeters? What can you do to let them know that God's forgiveness is available for all?

1. John Kramp, *Out of Their Faces and into Their Shoes* (Nashville: Broadman and Holman, 1995), 128.
2. John W. Eddins Jr. and J. Terry Young, *Holman Bible Dictionary* (Nashville: Holman Bible Publishers, 1991), 560.
3. Ibid., 560–61.

MY FAITH CONNECTIONS

Visitation Summary

Attempts _____

Completed visits _____

Key Question asked _____

Record a synopsis of your team's visits. Include actions you may need to take on needs discovered. Whom should you tell about these needs? Prayer partners? Sunday School teacher? Minister?

_____

_____

_____

_____

Life-Witness Summary

Key Question asked _____

_____

_____

_____

_____

My Journey This Week

What has God taught you this week? Records insights you have gained about God and yourself.

_____

_____

_____

_____

To-Do List

☐ Read session 5
☐ Completed "My FAITH Journey":
  ☐ Day 1
  ☐ Day 2
  ☐ Day 3
  ☐ Day 4
  ☐ Day 5

☐ Asked a friend or family member the Key Question
☐ Contacted prayer partners
☐ Memorized "I Is for *Impossible*" section of FAITH presentation
☐ Reviewed "F Is for *Forgiveness*" and "A Is for *Available*" sections of FAITH presentation
☐ _____
☐ _____
☐ _____
☐ _____
☐ _____
☐ _____

Prayer List

Lost people for whom you are praying:
☐ _____
☐ _____
☐ _____
☐ _____
☐ _____
☐ _____
☐ _____
☐ _____
☐ _____
☐ _____
☐ _____

Others needing prayer:
☐ _____
☐ _____
☐ _____
☐ _____
☐ _____
☐ _____
☐ _____
☐ _____

DAY 1

This week you learned that A is for *available* in the FAITH gospel presentation. Today let's build on what you have learned by preparing to examine the next letter in the outline, I is for *impossible*.

Review the characteristics of God on page 79. Now select some of the characteristics and rewrite them to describe people. For example:

God is _____Lord and Master_____.   People are __created and are worshipers__.

Now you try it.

God is _____.   People are _____.
God is _____.   People are _____.
God is _____.   People are _____.

Regardless of how you described humanity, an obvious gap exists between who God is and who we are. For example, consider our ability to determine the motives of people. At best we guess why a person does what he or she does. Even if someone tells you, you cannot be 100 percent sure that he is telling you every detail about his motives. God, on the other hand, knows everything. He is aware of every motive and the complexities of why we do what we do.

In ancient times the king was supreme. He had the best food, the best home, and the best amusements. If anyone wanted to approach a king, he or she had to wait to be invited, and even then there were no guarantees. When Queen Esther approached the king without an invitation, she risked death (see Esth. 4:11). In addition, in most realms individuals with physical challenges were not allowed in the presence of the king. That's why King David was considered magnanimous when he allowed Mephibosheth to eat at his table (see 2 Sam. 9:1-8). Although these practices appear cruel today, they were based on the concept that some people were not worthy of being in the king's presence.

Similarly, because of sin, no person is worthy of being in God's presence. In session 5 we discovered that God's forgiveness is not automatic. Only through Jesus can we approach God's throne. Some people with whom we are building relationships might wonder or ask why forgiveness is not automatic. The answer is found in the letter I of the FAITH gospel presentation.

I Is for *Impossible*

According to the Bible, it is impossible to get to heaven on our own.

*"By grace you are saved through faith, and this is not from yourselves;
it is God's gift—not from works, so that no one can boast."*
Ephesians 2:8-9

So how can a sinful person have eternal life and enter heaven?

Subsequent points in the outline will help you answer that question. In the meantime begin to memorize these statements and the Bible passage while continuing to review F and A in the FAITH gospel outline.

DAY 2

Imagine you are conducting Opinion Polls. When you knock on the door, the person who answers is the person you would least want to share Jesus with. Perhaps this person is known in the community to have a criminal record or a bad reputation. Perhaps the person's moral or social values conflict with yours. Perhaps it is someone with whom you have had a personal conflict in the past. Nevertheless, you begin to ask the questions on the survey, and he or she kindly answers. When asked the Key Question, he or she gives a vague faith answer but stops you from asking more about what his or her answers means. You express thanks for sharing and go on your way.

The next day your pastor calls you and wants to know more about the person you visited. After asking some general questions, your pastor asks you whether you would be willing to contact that person again and invite him or her to attend your Sunday School class with you.

What will you tell your pastor? _____

_____

_____

_____

_____

You could respond in a variety or ways, even refusing to help or suggesting that the person may feel more comfortable in another class. The fact remains that Jesus offers forgiveness to all. We must believe the gospel is for all and can make a difference in the life of even someone we despise. A wise pastor once said if we don't believe that the gospel is for everyone and that it can make a difference even in the life of a criminal, we ought to close our doors and go to work for a community-involvement organization.

Review "Getting Personal" on page 80. Stop and pray, confessing any prejudices against individuals or groups. Ask God to help you overcome your biases so that you can demonstrate His forgiveness-for-all attitude. What can you begin doing today to show these people that God's forgiveness is available for them?

_____

_____

_____

_____

_____

DAY 3

The Israelites had been captured and led off to Babylon. They had lost confidence in God, wondering why He was not able to defend them when the Babylonians arrived. In ancient times war was viewed as a test not only between nations but also between the deities of those nations. The nation that won was viewed as having the stronger and superior deity. When Babylon defeated Israel in 587 B.C., many probably viewed that defeat as proof that Bel and Marduk were superior to Yahweh. The Israelites seemed unable to understand that their own failure, not God's failure, was to blame for their exile. Feeling that God was going to leave them alone, most Israelites had turned to the idols of Babylon.

It was to this group of people that the prophet Isaiah directed these words:

> Zion, herald of good news,
> go up on a high mountain.
> Jerusalem, herald of good news,
> raise your voice loudly.
> Raise it, do not be afraid!
> Say to the cities of Judah,
> "Here is your God!"
> Isaiah 40:9

Isaiah was reintroducing the nation to God.

If you were introducing God to someone, what would you say? You may want to read how Isaiah did it in Isaiah 40.

_____

_____

_____

_____

_____

_____

If you asked people how they would describe God, you would get all kinds of answers. Most would say that God is love, a helper, or an avenger. Few would describe God as the One who will judge their lives by the standard of His Word. Review once again the characteristics of God on page 79.

Which characteristic comforts you the most? _____

Which makes you most uncomfortable? _____

Spend time with God today simply reading some psalms or proverbs. Ask God to help you understand Him in a new way. Record your insights in a journal or on this page.

DAY 4

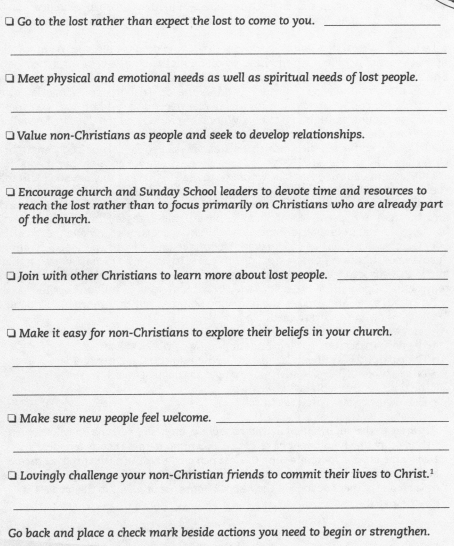

Review the way you marked the evaluation on page 78.

After each characteristic below, list ways you currently perform that action.

❑ Go to the lost rather than expect the lost to come to you. _____

_____

❑ Meet physical and emotional needs as well as spiritual needs of lost people.

_____

❑ Value non-Christians as people and seek to develop relationships.

_____

❑ Encourage church and Sunday School leaders to devote time and resources to reach the lost rather than to focus primarily on Christians who are already part of the church.

_____

❑ Join with other Christians to learn more about lost people. _____

_____

❑ Make it easy for non-Christians to explore their beliefs in your church.

_____

_____

❑ Make sure new people feel welcome. _____

_____

❑ Lovingly challenge your non-Christian friends to commit their lives to Christ.[1]

_____

Go back and place a check mark beside actions you need to begin or strengthen.

Share these characteristics with your prayer partners, asking them for their ideas and continued prayers on your behalf. Pray that God will help you demonstrate these qualities in an active, loving way.

1. John Kramp, *Out of Their Faces and into Their Shoes* (Nashville: Broadman and Holman, 1995), 128.

DAY 5

Last week we considered the highly receptive (U1) lost person (p. 74). Today we will examine the second group, lost persons who are characterized as receptive. Remember, the purpose of these research features is to better understand our world and to recognize that many people have an interest in learning more about Jesus. This information should encourage FAITH teams. Our responsibility is to be obedient as disciples and witnesses, relying on the Holy Spirit to do the work only He can do.

Leda is a 44-year-old stay-at-home mom. Having grown up going to church the first 14 years of her life, she remembers a lot about the youth events and the pastor. She also remembers that her father never attended church. She saw her dad as a good man who did just as much good as the churched people. One day after church, a deacon in the church told Leda she needed to get her dad to come to church so that he wouldn't go to hell. When she challenged the deacon, he walked away from the confrontation. Leda has not been to church since. She knows Jesus died on a cross for her sins, but she also believes people can be good enough to earn their way to heaven. Her position is understandable because her dad is now dead. For her to admit otherwise would be to realize that her dad is in hell and that the deacon was right.

Leda is a typical receptive lost person (U2, receptive as classified by Dr. Rainer and his research team). Most lost people in this category have some church background and understand some basic Christian doctrines but have the idea that people can work their way to heaven. Most have had a bad experience in church at some point. However, they are likely to come to Christ if we dialogue with them about the gospel. According to the research, this group, also known as seekers, represents 27 percent of the lost in the United States, or 43 million people.

Dr. Rainer's research makes the following points about this group of lost people.
- They are eager to study the Bible.
- They want to talk about eternal issues.
- They are frustrated by their understanding of works salvation.
- Their parents have been significant in their spiritual pilgrimage.
- Talking about their negative experiences in the past could open the door to future dialogue.
- They want to be invited to church.[1]

Put faces to this information as you review the names of persons on your prayer list. Identify any who might be receptive, according to these characteristics. Determine actions for addressing the lost persons' needs in each of the six areas suggested above by Dr. Rainer. Relying on the Holy Spirit's leadership, seek to take at least one of these actions in the next 48 hours. Be obedient to the way He is directing you.

1. Adapted from Thom S. Rainer, *The Unchurched Next Door* (Grand Rapids, MI: Zondervan, 2003), 165–66.

SESSION

I IS FOR *IMPOSSIBLE*

SESSION GOALS

You will—
- explore Scripture passages that reveal the nature of sin;
- examine the meaning of Ephesians 2:8-9 in the FAITH presentation;
- identify signs of a lost person's openness to the gospel;
- reflect on the things about which someone should boast.

According to the Bible, it is impossible to get to heaven on our own.

"By grace you are saved through faith, and this is not from yourselves; it is God's gift—not from works, so that no one can boast."
Ephesians 2:8-9

So how can a sinful person have eternal life and enter heaven?

As hard as we may try, some things are impossible for us to do.

What are some things you wish you could do but you know are impossible?

_____

_____

_____

_____

Each of the things you listed reminds us that people have _____.
We would like to think there are no limitations to what we can do, but experience teaches us otherwise. Some people waste their entire lives pursing things that are unachievable, unwilling to accept the limitations of their humanity. Doctors can do only so much to help the sick. All athletes retire and have a last game. Even Superman has to avoid kryptonite.

The letter *I* in the FAITH gospel presentation also reminds us that we have limitations. *I* stands for *impossible*. All people have fallen short of God's _____ for His creation. In previous sessions we have learned that we need God's forgiveness for sin and that His forgiveness and restoration are found in Jesus and Jesus alone. We have discovered that this forgiveness is available for all, but it is not automatic. During this session we will learn why it is impossible for us to attain _____ and _____ _____ on our own.

ON OUR OWN, HEAVEN IS IMPOSSIBLE

This is a startling statement, particularly for people who think their presumed innocence gets them into heaven. Many people automatically think heaven is the destination of everyone who has not committed the most horrible crimes. Think about the ways our culture refers to a deceased person: "up there," "at rest," or "with God." Some people casually refer to heaven as if it were their automatic destination when they die. *Certainly, God would not keep any good person out of heaven,* they seem to think.

However, the Bible says it is impossible for someone to go to heaven by their own _____ or to stand in God's presence by their own _____. There are two primary reasons this is true: (1) because of who _____ is and (2) because of who _____ are.

Look back at the characteristics of God we examined in the previous session (p. 79). God's supreme perfection dominates the list. We humans don't come close to God's character. When we compare God's perfection and holiness to our imperfection and sinfulness, we begin to recognize that we cannot have a right relationship with God unless something changes.

Because God is perfect, He cannot allow _____ or unredeemed _____ in His presence. Sin is part of our rebellious nature. An unredeemed person cannot help but sin. All of us are blemished to the point that we cannot be allowed, as we presently are, into God's presence. Sin is that serious. Sin _____ us from God. Sin is not only bad or wrong actions but also direct rebellion against God. In addition to doing wrong, failing to do the things we should do is sin as well: "For the person who knows to do good and doesn't do it, it is a sin" (Jas. 4:17).

Read the following passages. What does each one teach you about sin?

Psalm 73:3-19,27: _____

_____

_____

Psalm 94:1-7: _____

_____

_____

Isaiah 1:2-9: _____

_____

_____

Romans 3:10-18: _____

_____

_____

Galatians 5:19-21: _____

_____

_____

Colossians 3:5-10: _____

_____

_____

Titus 3:3: _____

_____

_____

THE IMPOSSIBLE MADE POSSIBLE

The verses used with *I* in the FAITH gospel presentation, Ephesians 2:8-9, explain how God makes possible what is impossible on our own.

According to the Bible, it is impossible to get to heaven on our own.

"By grace you are saved through faith, and this is not from yourselves;
it is God's gift—not from works, so that no one can boast."
Ephesians 2:8-9

If you carry a marked New Testament, this may be a good time to show the lost person these verses in your Bible. Someone who is not familiar with the Bible can see that everything you are sharing is indeed from God's Word.

Continue to rely completely on the Holy Spirit to discern and respond to the person with whom you are sharing. Many people are overwhelmed by problems for which they see no solution; yet they give no thought to heaven. As you begin to show the way God has made possible the impossible—through the forgiveness of sin and a personal relationship with the sovereign God of the universe—you offer _____, _____ , and _____ for the present as well as for eternity.

Record the first thoughts that come to your mind about each phrase in Ephesians 2:8-9.

By grace: _____

_____

_____

_____

You are saved: _____

_____

_____

_____

Through faith: _____

_____

_____

_____

And this is not from yourselves: _____

_____

_____

It is God's gift: _____

_____

_____

_____

Not from works: _____

_____

_____

_____

So that no one can boast: _____

_____

_____

_____

Let's explore what each phrase means.

1. By God's _____

From His grace alone God chose to act in history. Humanity rejected God's rule in this world and tried to replace it with our own power. We deserved death after failing in our quest to take over God's throne. He did not have to act on our behalf, but He chose to do so. He provided a sacrifice—His own Son—so that we could have forgiveness and a relationship with Him.

2. You are _____

Humanity was on a course leading to destruction. This destruction was complete, involving all areas of our lives and all creation. We needed to be rescued from ourselves. Through Jesus' death and resurrection, God delivered us from the penalty and power of sin. That deliverance is available to everyone.

3. Through _____

This rescue is not forced on us but is possible through our faith in God. As we discovered in session 5, God's forgiveness is not automatic. We must receive God's gift, acting on the offer He makes. We do so by placing our faith in Jesus alone (we will examine this topic in the next session).

4. Not of _____

Salvation is not a plan created in someone's mind. God did it; it is His plan. He is the One who convicts us of our sin and gives us the ability and opportunity to express faith in Him.

5. It is God's _____

As we discovered in John 3:16, God gave us His Son to be a sacrifice for sin in our place. Like any gift, His gift of forgiveness must be accepted to become reality. Gifts are free and are given with the intent that the recipient will enjoy and benefit from them. Once a gift is given, it becomes the property of the recipient. Salvation is God's gift that He allows us to possess.

6. Not from _____

We can do nothing to gain salvation. We can try all we want, but we cannot gain salvation on our own. Salvation is based completely on faith in Christ. Because no one can earn it, salvation is equally accessible to everyone through the same means, revealing God's wisdom and fairness.

7. So that no one can _____

Only God can receive the credit and glory for our salvation. Even our best accomplishment is inferior to God's least accomplishment. The psalmist declared:

> I will praise the LORD at all times;
> His praise will always be on my lips.
> I will boast in the LORD;
> the humble will hear and be glad.
> Proclaim with me the LORD's greatness;
> let us exalt His name together.
> I sought the LORD, and He answered me
> and delivered me from all my fears.
> Those who look to Him are radiant with joy;
> their faces will never be ashamed.
> This poor man cried, and the LORD heard him
> and saved him from all his troubles.
> Psalm 34:1-6

Because God accomplished salvation for us, we can boast only in Him, giving Him all the honor and praise He is due.

While the Key Question allows you to initiate a conversation about spiritual things with a lost person, at this point in the presentation you must ask a second question:

So how can a sinful person have eternal life and enter heaven?

If you have been dialoguing with a person, having already shared F and A, a nonbeliever may have recognized for the first time the impossible situation he is in. Asking the question "So how can a sinful person have eternal life and enter heaven?" can reinforce this truth and open the opportunity to share God's solution, which we will examine in the next session.

OPPORTUNITIES FOR CONTINUED DIALOGUE

When you present the FAITH gospel presentation, *I* is for *impossible* may introduce issues like the following that you will need to address.

1. Respond to the claim that we can _____ heaven.

You have likely already encountered, and will continue to meet, people who see themselves as good, moral individuals. Some think they have not sinned because they do not commit serious or harmful acts. In their understanding of what sin is, they are sinless. This view is contrary to biblical teaching.

You might share three general categories of sin (commission, omission, and secret) from session 4 (see p. 67) to help lost persons understand that they have sinned. In addition, Jesus taught that anger is as much a sin as murder and that lust is as much a sin as adultery (see Matt. 5:21-22,27-28). James stated, "Whoever keeps the entire law, yet fails in one point, is guilty of breaking it all" (Jas. 2:10). The Bible teaches that a person has to break only one of God's laws one time to be guilty. Therefore, everyone has _____ in some way and is incapable of being _____ _____ to achieve heaven.

2. Be sensitive to _____ signals.

Dr. Rainer discovered that 38 percent of the unchurched are either friendly or very friendly to the gospel.[1] The groups we have reviewed the past two weeks in day 5 of "My FAITH Journey" are open, often seeking the truth and willing to talk with someone. When these people take a step of action in their spiritual searches, they do not carry a sign reading, "Don't miss me. I'm ready to talk about God." Usually, indicators of spiritual interest are subtle. The following signals may indicate someone's desire to engage in dialogue with you about spiritual things.

- *Asking* _____. Pay attention to any question that relates to spiritual matters. Lost persons do not ask questions about the Bible or about church because they are suddenly curious. The questions reveal spiritual activity in their lives.
- *Attending* _____. A lost person's attendance at church is always significant. Christians should assume that God is at work in the person's life.
- *Reading the* _____ *or religious* _____. Pay attention when lost persons tell you they are reading the Bible or a religious book. What they are willing to read indicates a need in their lives and perhaps a willingness to talk about spiritual matters.
- *Viewing or listening to Christian* _____. When non-Christians mention a Christian podcast, radio broadcast, CD, DVD, or TV program, ask follow-up questions. Ask them to tell you about the speaker's message. Find out what they thought about the program.
- *Participating in Christian* _____ _____. If lost persons join Christians in an activity, such as recreation or a ministry project, the event has spiritual significance. They evaluate Christians they meet in an informal setting to see what, if anything, is distinctive about their lives.

GETTING PERSONAL

It is virtually impossible for unsaved persons to be open to the gospel until they understand that they are _____ who need _____. Romans 3:10 states, "There is no one righteous, not even one." When we identify ourselves with the truth of this verse, it makes it easier for the lost person to see himself in that same condition. Be very careful when you are sharing *I* is for *impossible* that you do not come across as _____. Until you chose God's way over your own, you were just as guilty.

When we have a role to play in a person's accepting Christ, it is easy to feel superior to others who have not yet had that experience. Paul reminded the Ephesians that they had no reason to boast about being a Christian. The apostle also proclaimed to the Galatian believers that "as for me, I will never boast about anything except the cross of our Lord Jesus Christ, through whom the world has been crucified to me, and I to the world" (Gal 6:14). Because it is God's salvation, He gets the _____. We just happen to be there when God is doing His work.

What can you do to boast about God today? How can you give God credit for the things He is doing in, through, and around you?

_____

_____

_____

_____

_____

_____

_____

1. Thom S. Rainer, *The Unchurched Next Door* (Grand Rapids, MI: Zondervan, 2003), 23.

MY FAITH CONNECTIONS

Visitation Summary

Attempts _____
Completed visits _____
Key Question asked _____

Record a synopsis of your team's visits. Include actions you may need to take on needs discovered. Whom should you tell about these needs? Prayer partners? Sunday School teacher? Minister?

_____

_____

_____

_____

Life-Witness Summary

Key Question asked _____

_____

_____

_____

_____

My Journey This Week

What has God taught you this week? Records insights you have gained about God and yourself.

_____

_____

_____

_____

To-Do List

- ☐ Read session 6
- ☐ Completed "My FAITH Journey":
  - ☐ Day 1
  - ☐ Day 2
  - ☐ Day 3
  - ☐ Day 4
  - ☐ Day 5

- ☐ Completed evangelistic story
- ☐ Contacted prayer partners
- ☐ Memorized "T Is for *Turn*" section of FAITH presentation
- ☐ Reviewed "F Is for *Forgiveness*," "A Is for *Available*," and "I Is for *Impossible*" sections of FAITH presentation
- ☐ _____
- ☐ _____
- ☐ _____
- ☐ _____
- ☐ _____
- ☐ _____

Prayer List

Lost people for whom you are praying:
- ☐ _____
- ☐ _____
- ☐ _____
- ☐ _____
- ☐ _____
- ☐ _____
- ☐ _____
- ☐ _____
- ☐ _____
- ☐ _____
- ☐ _____

Others needing prayer:
- ☐ _____
- ☐ _____
- ☐ _____
- ☐ _____
- ☐ _____
- ☐ _____
- ☐ _____
- ☐ _____
- ☐ _____

DAY 1

MY FAITH JOURNEY

This week you learned that *I* is for *impossible* in the FAITH gospel presentation. Today let's build on what you have learned by preparing to examine the next letter in the outline, *T* is for *turn*.

Brenda is trying to memorize the FAITH presentation. She hands her daughter a copy of the outline and asks her to check her memorization. When Brenda asks, "Would you like to receive God's forgiveness?" her daughter, in tears, looks at her mother and emphatically answers, "Yes!"

Ben is a paroled felon in your city, having been to jail several times. During a worship service he sits beside you. Afterward he asks you questions about spiritual matters. You get his name and address so that your FAITH team can visit him. While visiting with him, you take advantage of an opportunity to share the FAITH gospel presentation. After several conversations Ben commits his life to Christ.

Marc, a mentally challenged member of your church, can communicate on a limited basis. A friend of yours, who teaches Marc's Sunday School class, tells you that Marc is asking many spiritual questions. Your friend invites you to go visit Marc with him. Marc indicates that he is a sinner who needs Jesus. In his own way Marc asks Jesus to forgive him. He asks you and your friend to help him into the baptistery and to stand beside him as he is baptized.

These three persons, while different in obvious ways, are also the same: they all realized that they could not earn their way into heaven and needed to turn to Jesus. It is a special experience to see someone realize that he or she needs Jesus. You will not soon forget the look in their eyes or the anticipation in your heart as friends or acquaintances begin to turn toward Jesus.

By the next session you will be responsible for having memorized the FAITH presentation through *T* is for *turn*.

T Is for *Turn*
Question: If you were going down the road and someone asked you to turn, what would he or she be asking you to do? *(Change direction)*
Turn means *repent*.

Turn away from sin and self.
"Unless you repent, you will all perish as well!"
Luke 13:3

Turn to Jesus alone as your Savior and Lord.
"I am the way, the truth, and the life. No one comes to the Father except through Me."
John 14:6

Here is the greatest news of all.
"If you confess with your mouth, 'Jesus is Lord,' and believe in your heart that God raised Him from the dead, you will be saved. With the heart one believes, resulting in righteousness, and with the mouth one confesses, resulting in salvation."
Romans 10:9-10

Begin to memorize these statements and Bible passages. As you do so, continue to review the F, A, and I sections of the FAITH gospel outline. Most of all, pray that God will plant the presentation in your heart and will give you the sensitivity and opportunity to share.

DAY 2

During this week's session we reviewed several passages that describe the condition of a person who is dominated by sin (p. 89). The last passage listed was from the pen of Paul. Reminding one of his young protégés to remember what life was like without Jesus, Paul stated, "We too were once foolish, disobedient, deceived, captives of various passions and pleasures, living in malice and envy, hateful, detesting one another" (Titus 3:3). Paul similarly described a life of sin when he wrote to the Ephesians (see Eph. 2:1-4) and the Colossians (see Col. 3:5-10).

It is noteworthy that Paul included himself in this group. Prior to becoming a follower of Jesus, Paul, then known as Saul, was a strict Pharisee. As such, he would have been a keeper of the law, at least outwardly. Paul claimed that he had been blameless in keeping the Jewish laws (see Phil 3:6). If anyone had a right to claim that he could earn his way to heaven, it would have been Paul. Yet Paul realized that his efforts to keep the Jewish law came up short.

Paul wrote the words of Ephesians 2:8-9. He knew, both from experience and from God's Word, that no one can earn his way to heaven.

Consider your own life for a moment. Could it be said of you that you are blameless? ☐ Yes ☐ No

What additional sins might you have added to Paul's list if you had written that letter to Titus?

_____

_____

_____

_____

_____

As you go through this day, thank God for providing Jesus, who made it possible for you to do the impossible—to be saved and to have a personal relationship with Him.

DAY 3

Over the past six weeks we have prayed for persons we regularly come in contact with, asking God to help us engage them in spiritual dialogue. By now you may have had the opportunity at least to enter a dialogue with one or more of these people.

Session 6 identified five seeker signals to be aware of when you talk with lost persons (p. 93). Some of the persons on your prayer list in "My FAITH Connections" weekly checklist most likely show evidence of interest in spiritual things.

On the chart below, indicate the seeker signals you have observed in the persons for whom you have been praying. Write the names of the persons in the left column and check the signals they have displayed.

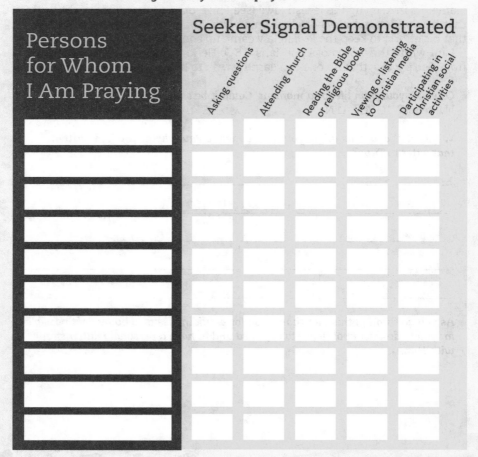

Persons for Whom I Am Praying	Seeker Signal Demonstrated				
	Asking questions	Attending church	Reading the Bible or religious books	Viewing or listening to Christian media	Participating in Christian social activities

Focus on the individuals who exhibit the most readiness and interest in the gospel. Pray especially for them today, asking God for the opportunity to share with them within the next 48 hours. Ask your prayer partners to keep you in their prayers during this time.

DAY 4

Someone can do the right things for the wrong reasons and still be wrong. God is interested in the reason we do something just as much as in what we actually do. Too many times Christians practice works salvation. For example, they may have these thoughts or use these words:

- "I can't stop teaching this class. If I do, I will need to do something else to stay in good standing."
- "Sure, I tithe; I don't want God to 'zap' me."
- "If I invite enough people to church, it will give me one more safety net to get into heaven."

Behind each statement is the idea that we can earn our way to heaven. These actions are good, but they cannot earn a free ticket to heaven. But before we throw stones, let's look at our own lives.

Why do you do the things you do for the Lord? What motivates you in Kingdom service? Take time to reflect on why you are involved in the things you are involved in. Then check one of the following.

☐ *My good works are a result of God's work in my life.*

☐ *I am trying to prove my worthiness.*

Ask God to help you correct any wrong motives.

If you serve God to gain or prove something, you will eventually lose the joy of serving. You will find true freedom when you do things, including FAITH, to express your love for God.

When you do something for someone you love, you don't view it as work or with disgust. Instead, you look forward to it because you get an opportunity to show that person how much you care. In the same way, when you serve God from love, you will also discover the pure joy of service.

DAY 5

Today we will examine the lost who are classified as neutral (U3) in Thom Rainer's research. Here is a sample of what you might encounter when dialoguing with a neutral lost person.

Todd: What is your religious background?
Paul: Methodist.
Todd: Would you like to elaborate?
Paul: No.
Todd: What should churches do to attract more people?
Paul: Nothing.
Todd: Do you pray to God on a regular basis?
Paul: No.
Todd: If you decided to go to church, what day would you prefer?
Paul: Sunday.
Todd: Do you believe heaven exists?
Paul: Yes.
Todd: How about hell?
Paul: Yes.
Todd: What do you believe about Jesus Christ?
Paul: God exists.
Todd: Who has been the greatest influence in your life?
Paul: Grandparents.
Todd: Can you tell us more about them?
Paul: No.
Todd: Has anyone ever shared with you how to become a Christian?
Paul: No.
Todd: If someone invited you to attend church, would you go?
Paul: No.[1]

Neutral lost people are not neutral in terms of an opinion but in terms of a commitment. They have an opinion, but they don't want to make a commitment about Christianity one way or the other. Some are leaning toward Christianity, while others are leaning away from it. They simply have not decided for themselves yet.

A little more than one-third (36 percent) of the lost people interviewed fell into this—roughly 19 million Americans.[2] Most U3s or neutrals interviewed indicated that they would attend church if another person invited them and picked them up. They are not closed to discussion or even to the church; instead, they are neutral—in the process of making a decision.

1. Thom S.. Rainer, *The Unchurched Next Door* (Grand Rapids, MI: Zondervan, 2003), 131–33.
2. Ibid., 132.

SESSION

T IS FOR *TURN*

SESSION GOALS

You will—
- understand the concept of repentance in terms of turning;
- realize that repentance has always been part of God's plan;
- characterize Jesus as the only way to heaven;
- identify what a person must do to receive salvation.

Question: If you were going down the road and someone asked you to turn, what would he or she be asking you to do? *(Change direction)*

Turn means *repent.*

Turn away from sin and self.

"Unless you repent, you will all perish as well!"
Luke 13:3

Turn to Jesus alone as your Savior and Lord.

"I am the way, the truth, and the life. No one comes to the Father except through Me."
John 14:6

Here is the greatest news of all.

"If you confess with your mouth, 'Jesus is Lord,' and believe in your heart that God raised Him from the dead, you will be saved. With the heart one believes, resulting in righteousness, and with the mouth one confesses, resulting in salvation."
Romans 10:9-10

Imagine it is halftime at a college football game. The teams have jogged off to their locker rooms, and the band is getting ready to take the field. Each instrumentalist, twirler, flag bearer, and drum major has taken his or her position. The drum line begins moving forward in perfect rhythm, with the band following. They play and move from one position to another up and down the field.

When they hit their marks, each person turns in just the right way to avoid the other band members. Each choreographed turn leads to the formation of another shape or symbol. As the halftime show comes to a conclusion, the band has formed the school logo. The band begins to play the school fight song, bringing audience members to their feet.

A good band can make nearly anyone wait to get that hotdog until after halftime. The secret is in the turns. Without the turns the band would simply stand and play. The movement is the element that makes fans stay in the stands during halftime. If the band failed to make a turn during the performance, everyone would end up in disarray. It's all about the turns!

In this session we will examine the letter *T* in the FAITH presentation. *T* is for *turn.* It is the turn that makes the difference.

THE SCRIPTURAL PICTURE OF TURNING

Most of the Old Testament was written in Hebrew; the New Testament, in Greek. Both languages use simple, beautiful images to depict abstract concepts. Turning is a significant image in Scripture and a significant action in the salvation experience.

God wants us to have a fulfilled life, to be what He created us to be. We have already discovered that He offers forgiveness to all people but that His forgiveness is not automatic. Furthermore, we have discovered that our sinfulness makes it impossible, on our own, to have a right relationship with God and to spend eternity in His presence. God chose to intervene, giving us a choice to make.

Our choice is a simple one: we can keep trusting _____ and living the way we are living, or we can give our lives to _____ and begin to follow

Him. Everyone must make his or her own choice. This choice is the most important decision anyone has faced or will face throughout history.

A number of Scripture passages use vivid imagery to depict turning from sin and self and turning to God through Christ alone for forgiveness and eternal life (repentance):

- Isaiah 45:20-22 contrasts idols and the true God. We are to turn from idols to God to be saved.
- Isaiah 55:7 paints a vivid picture of turning from unrighteousness and turning to the Lord for mercy and pardon.
- Ezekiel 33:10-11 indicates that God takes no pleasure in the deaths of the wicked; rather, He wants them to turn from their sin and live.
- Acts 3:19 makes it clear that we are to "repent and turn back, that your sins may be wiped out."
- Peter (in 1 Pet. 3:10-11) quoted from Psalm 34:12-16 to encourage people to turn away from evil.

God's messengers have always carried the same message: turn from sin and turn to God. Turning to _____ has been, is, and will always be the only _____ anyone has.

CHANGING DIRECTION

When you share the FAITH gospel presentation with a lost person, you will use a question to introduce the idea of turning.

> **Question: If you were going down the road and someone asked you to turn, what would he or she be asking you to do?** *(Change direction)*

> *Turn* **means** *repent.*

The idea of turning a car around is a common experience for most people. For many lost persons, pointing out the need to change direction while driving or riding in a car will communicate being lost or on the wrong path. You are trying to help them understand the need to change _____ in their lives or to get on the right _____. (If you are conversing with a marathon runner, a walker, or a jogger, referring to these activities instead of driving can help the person better understand the important concept of turning.)

At this point in the FAITH gospel presentation the lost person may recognize the Holy Spirit's convicting of sin and a personal need for God. *To turn* means *to _____ or to _____ that one is a sinner.* The turning analogy allows you to address the lost person's need to change direction.

Asking this question at this point in the presentation is also strategic because you are anticipating a response. You are inviting the individual to participate in the conversation. If questions have not yet come up as you have shared, asking this question gives you a way to find out whether the person is following what you are saying.

Remember the marching band at halftime? When the band members turn and march toward the opposite end of the field, they change their direction. Repentance carries the same idea: we turn away from our current path and begin going in another direction. To turn is a very straightforward image. We are to turn—repent—change the _____ of our lives.

Any turn has two parts.

1. Turn from _____ and _____.

Turn away from sin and self.
"Unless you repent, you will all perish as well!"
Luke 13:3

When we repent, we begin by turning from a life of sin and self. We stop trusting in our own merit and abilities. We realize that our own effort will not be enough to make us acceptable to God; therefore, self cannot be trusted. We also realize that our fundamental problem is sin, which separates us from God, and that we must no longer embrace a sinful way of life.

2. Turn to _____ _____.

Turn to Jesus alone as your Savior and Lord.
"I am the way, the truth, and the life. No one comes to the Father except through Me."
John 14:6

We also realize that we cannot let go of our sin on our own and that we need help. Jesus came to release us from the grip of sin (see Rev. 1:5). When we turn from sin and self and turn to Jesus, our expression of faith actualizes Jesus' work in our lives, making it possible for us to let go and embrace Him instead of our old, sinful ways. Turning from sin and self happens simultaneously with turning toward a new direction. We turn to Someone—to Jesus Christ only, in whom we put our trust.

In Acts 17 we find an interesting account that could take place in our world today. Paul was visiting the city of Athens. Athens was a very religious city, with a temple on every corner. Almost all religions were practiced there. A shrine that had been erected to an unknown god captured Paul's attention (see Acts 17:22-23). The people of Athens apparently wanted to make sure they had all the bases covered when honoring religions and deities. For them it didn't matter who or what people worshiped as long as they worshiped something.

Does this sound familiar? We live in a time when people are religious but misguided. Many religions and spiritual systems are practiced in our world today. If a person wants to believe something, he can find a group that believes it. Another dangerous action is accepting any and every belief. Other people choose various beliefs from different religions, creating their own personal religion. They choose the parts they like and ignore the elements that make them uncomfortable. This trend is nothing new. Isaiah challenged the people in his day to examine the idols they were adding to their worship. They hadn't abandoned God; they just began viewing Him as one of many. Isaiah pointed out that these other idols were simple pieces of wood and metal that were dead and had no power (see Isa. 40:18-26). This is still true. There is only one living God. There is no other.

As much as a person may want or try, he or she will not find multiple _____ leading to heaven. There is only one way, and that way is _____. Jesus was direct and clear when he declared Himself as the only way to the Father (see John 14:6). Jesus' declaration was full of meaning. Consider the ways Jesus is the way, the truth, and the life.

He is the _____—
• by His doctrine (see John 6:68);
• by His example (see 1 Pet. 2:21);
• by His sacrifice (see Heb. 9:8-9);
• by His Spirit (see John 16:13).

He is the _____—
- in opposition to all false religions (see John 1:14,17; 8:32);
- in contrast to the Mosaic law, which was only the shadow, not the truth or substance, of the good things that were to come (see Heb. 10:1-10);
- in respect to all the promises of God (see 2 Cor. 1:20).

He is the _____—
- that saves from death (see Rom. 8:1-2);
- that destroys death's power (see 1 Cor. 15:54-57);
- as the One who gives life (see John 11:25-26).

The bottom line is that Jesus and only Jesus is the way to God. Jesus is the only One capable of making the claim and backing it up with action. To some this truth may seem to be a narrow assertion, but it is fair. The path is the same for everyone, regardless of where they live or what they do. That path is Jesus.

THE GREATEST NEWS OF ALL

Here is the greatest news of all.
"If you confess with your mouth, 'Jesus is Lord,' and believe in your heart that God raised Him from the dead, you will be saved. With the heart one believes, resulting in righteousness, and with the mouth one confesses, resulting in salvation."
Romans 10:9-10

We know (or at some point tried to learn) that the area of a circle can be found by multiplying pi (π = approximately 3.14) by the square of the radius (the distance from the middle point of the circle to the outer edge). If a circle has a radius of 4, its area is about 50.24. We also know that a circle's circumference (the distance around the circle) can be found by multiplying pi (π) by the diameter of the circle, which is twice the length of the radius. If a circle has a diameter of 4, its circumference is about 12.56. These formulas remind us that some things in life are universally true. When we were in school, someone instructed us in how to use these formulas and apply them to specific situations.

The same is true of the way people enter a relationship with God through faith in Jesus Christ. In Romans 10 Paul explained how to apply the gospel message to our lives. He pointed to two actions that are required for a person to be saved.

1. _____ with your mouth.
The first action is confession. Confession is an admission, declaration, or acknowledgment. It involves both the confession of _____ and the confession of _____. Numerous Old Testament passages stress the importance of the confession of sin within the experience of worship. For example, presenting a sin offering and releasing a scapegoat that represented the removal of sin were acts of confession carried out in a worship experience (see Lev. 5:5—6:7; 16:20-22). In addition, confession was and continues to be a sinner's individual acknowledgment of sin (see Ps. 32:5; Prov. 28:13).

At the Jordan River John's followers were baptized, confessing their sins (see Matt. 3:6) Christians are reminded that God faithfully forgives the sins of those who confess them (see 1 John 1:9). James directed his readers to confess their sins to one another, most likely in the context of congregational worship (see Jas. 5:16).

When you share with someone about Christ, remember that the individual must come to a personal awareness that he has broken God's laws and has sinned against Him. He is confessing—admitting, declaring, acknowledging—that he is a sinner who needs Christ.

The other side of confession is a confession of faith, which is closely related to confession of sin. In 1 Kings 8:33,35 the acknowledgment of the name of God resulted in the forgiveness of sins. Someone's public acknowledgment of Jesus is the basis for Jesus' acknowledgment of that believer to God (see Matt. 10:32).

Confession includes both turning from sin and self and turning to Jesus alone, which are presented in the first part of *T is for turn*. We are to change our allegiance from trusting _____ and choosing _____, and we are to confess our new allegiance of trusting and following _____.

2. _____ in your heart.

The second action Paul identified in Romans 10:9-10 is to believe. To believe in someone is more than believing facts about them; it is a _____ of one person to another. When someone believes in Jesus, that person is confessing _____ to Him. Faith is a break from the past and all other religious allegiances (see 1 Thess. 1:9) and the beginning of a relationship with God. Faith, especially in Paul's letters, is the inauguration of incorporation in Christ, in which a believer continues to grow and develop.

Our English word *faith* comes from the Latin word *fides*. In Middle English (1150–1475) *faith* replaced a word that eventually evolved into *belief*. *Faith* came to mean *loyalty to a person to whom one is bound by promise or duty*. The concept of believing in or faith primarily refers to a personal relationship with God that determines the priorities of someone's life. This relationship is one of love that is built on _____ and _____. Faith is the acceptance of Christ's _____ or absolute authority over our lives.

Those who confess and believe will be _____. *Saved* is Paul's description of a person who commits his or her life to Jesus. It is an action performed by God. Being saved is the acutely dynamic act of snatching others by force from serious peril, usually in a life-or-death struggle. In its most basic sense, being saved or salvation is the saving of a life from _____ _____. Someone is no longer lost but is now saved, secure in the arms of God.

This is what is promised to those who are willing to confess Jesus as Lord and to believe in their hearts. When sharing with another person, you may want to emphasize the hope presented in Romans 10:9-10. Paul left little doubt about the outcome for those who are willing to commit their lives to Christ: they will be saved!

After you have shared verses on turning from sin and turning to Christ only, ask:

What happens if a person is willing to repent of their sins and confess Christ?

This question will help you find out whether the person understands what you have shared. The response may also give you some clues about the person's readiness to make a decision for Christ. This question also serves as a transition into *H is for heaven*, which we will examine in the next session.

CELEBRATING THE TURN

Interestingly, Jesus' parables on lostness in Luke 15 have celebration as a central theme. When the shepherd found the missing sheep, he celebrated with friends and neighbors (see vv. 5-6). The woman, on finding her coin, called her friends and neighbors together and said, "Rejoice with me, because I have found the silver coin I lost!" (v. 9). On his son's return, the father instructed his servants, " 'Quick! Bring out the best robe and put it on him; put a ring on his finger and sandals on his feet. Then bring the fattened calf and slaughter it, and let's celebrate with a feast, because this son of mine was dead and is alive again; he was lost and is found!' So they began to celebrate" (vv. 22-24).

Jesus left no doubt: when the lost are found, _____ occurs in heaven. What happens on earth should mirror the heavenly party in spirit and joy. If you have the privilege of being part of the Holy Spirit's leading someone to accept Christ, celebrate with the new believer and with those who have been praying. Thank God for allowing you to have a _____ in accomplishing His Great Commission.

OPPORTUNITIES FOR CONTINUED DIALOGUE

When you present the FAITH gospel presentation, *T* is for *turn* may present opportunities to discuss these related issues with the lost person.

1. _____ about Jesus
When you talk with lost persons, you will encounter a number of misconceptions about who Jesus is. Some people view Him as merely a miracle worker, a great person, an esteemed teacher, the founder of Christianity, a leader of the Jews, or a great prophet. While all of these characteristics are true, they do not fully describe who Jesus is—the only Son of God, fully human and fully divine. Scripture affirms Jesus to be virgin-born (see Matt. 1:18); tempted while on earth just as we are, yet sinless (see Heb. 4:15); the Sacrifice who made possible our salvation through His death on the cross (see 1 Cor. 15:3b); and our risen Lord (see 1 Cor. 15:4a). He intercedes for us even now (see Rom. 8:34) and promises to come again for us (see Acts 1:11).

Although you may not be able to explain all of the significant biblical doctrines, someone who trusts Jesus is expressing belief that He is who He says He is—the _____ of God and the only One who is able to _____. A person who trusts Christ believes what Jesus taught about His dying on our behalf, being raised by God from the dead, and returning in glory to claim us as His own for eternity.

2. A question about the _____ of those who never hear about Jesus
You can respond to such a question in several ways.
1. Affirm the person asking this question for thinking about others and everyone's need to know about Jesus.
2. Explain that the Bible reveals that God is just, righteous, and holy. Although God wants everyone to be saved (see 2 Pet. 3:9), His justice, righteousness, and holiness demand that He _____ the sin of those who do not accept His offer of salvation.
3. The Bible is not silent on the issue of those who have not heard about Jesus. Paul directly addressed the issue: "From the creation of the world His [God's] invisible attributes, that is, His eternal power and divine nature, have been clearly seen, being understood through what He has made. As a result, people are without excuse" (Rom. 1:20). Later Paul explained that those who have never heard the law of God will be judged according to the law that is written in their hearts (see Rom. 2:11-16). The law written in their hearts is the knowledge of right and wrong that is part of our human makeup. These verses indicate that God has revealed Himself to all humanity and that people will be held _____ for the revelation they have received.
4. Most people who ask this question are trying to justify their own standard for getting into heaven. Others use it to direct the conversation away from their

personal responsibility and sin. You might want to remind lost persons who raise this question that because they have heard the gospel, they will be judged by their response. Remind them that forgiveness though Jesus is being offered to them and that they must decide their response to God's offer. Rejecting Jesus brings God's judgment.

5. We can be sure that God's judgment of each person will be _____ and _____. We know that God is just and righteous and that what He does will be consistent with His character.

GETTING PERSONAL

Because Christians are not immune to _____, turning away from sin is a _____ _____ for a believer. Paul's call to flee youthful lusts (temptations) was directed to Timothy, a minister Paul was mentoring (see 2 Tim. 2:22). Every day we must remain on guard for the temptations that come our way. Satan loves nothing more than to see a Christian fail morally. God continues to offer us forgiveness if we fail (see 1 John 1:9, a verse addressed to believers), but that is not an excuse to continue living a life that dishonors God's name. We have a new life to live that is set apart and is no longer dominated by sin (see Rom. 6:1-4).

The reality is that someone out there is watching you. Unbelievers want to know whether your faith in Jesus makes a difference in this world. They want to observe the way you respond to the pressures of daily life, to the meanness of this world, and to disappointment. Strangely, deep down they hope your faith is real.

Being a witness is a _____ thing. The story is told of a man who was out for lunch with work associates. Everyone else ordered alcoholic beverages. It would have been easy for the man to order a drink without the alcohol or to get what everyone else ordered. Instead, he ordered tea, and his work associates teased him about it. The waitress even got into the game by "accidentally" placing one of the other men's drinks in front of him. Everyone had a laugh, but the man passed the drink on and grabbed his glass of tea. That night the man went out with his FAITH team doing Opinion Polls. As they knocked on the first door, both he and the person opening the door were surprised because they recognized each other. It was the waitress from lunch.

Suppose the man had chosen to go along with his associates and had gotten just one alcoholic drink. How do you think the waitress would have responded when he introduced himself as being from a church? Remember, the lost want something that works, and most hope you can show them that Jesus is what they have been looking for.

God has a _____ for intersecting our lives with others. We may never know the difference we make by living a life that matches our faith claims. To do that, we have to turn our backs on the temptations that come our way and continually _____ to Christ in faith and dependence.

As you go through the next week, think about things in your life that could be stumbling blocks to someone who is considering Christ. Write actions you may need to take to turn to Christ when tempted and not give in to your weaknesses.

_____

_____

_____

MY FAITH CONNECTIONS

Visitation Summary

Attempts _____
Completed visits _____
Key Question asked _____

Record a synopsis of your team's visits. Include actions you may need to take on needs discovered. Whom should you tell about these needs? Prayer partners? Sunday School teacher? Minister?

_____

_____

_____

_____

Life-Witness Summary

Key Question asked _____

_____

_____

_____

_____

My Journey This Week

What has God taught you this week? Records insights you have gained about God and yourself.

_____

_____

_____

_____

To-Do List

☐ Read session 7
☐ Completed "My FAITH Journey":
  ☐ Day 1
  ☐ Day 2
  ☐ Day 3
  ☐ Day 4
  ☐ Day 5

☐ Contacted prayer partners
☐ Memorized "H Is for *Heaven*" section of FAITH presentation
☐ Reviewed "F Is for *Forgiveness*," "A Is for *Available*," "I Is for *Impossible*," and "T Is for *Turn*" sections of FAITH presentation
☐ _____
☐ _____
☐ _____
☐ _____
☐ _____
☐ _____

Prayer List

Lost people for whom you are praying:
☐ _____
☐ _____
☐ _____
☐ _____
☐ _____
☐ _____
☐ _____
☐ _____
☐ _____
☐ _____

Others needing prayer:
☐ _____
☐ _____
☐ _____
☐ _____
☐ _____
☐ _____
☐ _____
☐ _____
☐ _____

DAY 1

This week you learned that T is for *turn* in the FAITH gospel presentation. Today let's build on what you have learned by preparing to examine the next letter in the outline, H is for *heaven*.

Heaven. Just the word itself sounds good. Delightful images rush through our minds when we hear or see the word. A smile comes across our faces. Heaven is where everything is the way it is supposed to be. There we will be able to fulfill completely our purpose in God's creation.

What images come to your mind when you think of heaven? _____

_____

God wants us to begin experiencing heaven now. Because Jesus lives in our hearts, we don't have to wait to live with purpose and to enjoy fellowship with God. Although life on earth will never be all God intended it to be, we can begin to get a taste of life in heaven as we experience God here on earth.

One way we can have heaven on earth is to spend time with God now. He wants to tell us great truths about Himself, and He wants to start teaching them to us now. Jeremiah was reminded of this fact as he sat in house arrest (see Jer. 33:1-3). Peter knew the peace of heaven as he rested even while chained to two prison guards (see Acts 12:1-6). Because we are God's children, heaven is what we desire, and it is the state for which we were created.

Having shared with a person about forgiveness and the need to repent, you will then focus on the results of that repentance. The results are heaven and eternal life. By the next session you will be responsible for having memorized the final letter in the FAITH outline, H is for *heaven*.

What happens if a person is willing to repent of their sins and confess Christ?

_____

H Is for *Heaven*

Heaven is a place where we will live with God forever.
"If I go away and prepare a place for you, I will come back and receive you to Myself, so that where I am you may be also."
John 14:3

Eternal life begins now with Jesus.
"I have come that they may have life and have it in abundance."
John 10:10

H can also stand for *how*.

How can a person have God's forgiveness, eternal life, and heaven?
By trusting Jesus as your Savior and Lord.

Continue reviewing the first four letters in the FAITH gospel presentation.

DAY 2

Sin is ugly, and it happens in the lives of even the people we least expect to give in to it. David, a great king who was in tune with God, had an adulterous affair. When the other man's wife, Bathsheba, became pregnant, David tried to cover up his sin. As a last resort he ordered his generals to place Bathsheba's husband, Uriah, in the fiercest military battle. Uriah was killed, and Bathsheba became David's wife. David thought he had gotten away with it until a prophet named Nathan confronted him (see 2 Sam. 12).

While many consequences resulted from this sin or series of sins, the most serious was the effect it had on the relationship between David and God. David knew he had sinned against God (see Ps. 51:3-4). Because David had demonstrated great confidence in God throughout his life, God had honored him. David had a deep friendship with God, and now that friendship was damaged. In Psalm 51 David put into words the feelings he experienced. David's response was one of repentance.

Read these words from Psalm 51. Circle or underline words or phrases that point to David's desire to change direction or to repent.

> Purify me with hyssop, and I will be clean;
> wash me, and I will be whiter than snow.
> Let me hear joy and gladness;
> let the bones You have crushed rejoice.
> Turn Your face away from my sins
> and blot out all my guilt.
> God, create a clean heart for me
> and renew a steadfast spirit within me.
> Do not banish me from Your presence
> or take Your Holy Spirit from me.
> Restore the joy of Your salvation to me,
> and give me a willing spirit.
> Then I will teach the rebellious Your ways,
> and sinners will return to You.
> Psalm 51:7-13

Reflect on David's words throughout this day. Make them your own words, asking God to do the same thing in your life. Ask God to help you live a life that honors Him.

DAY 3

Brazil is the home to a unique prison called Humaita, located in Sao Jose de Campos. The prison, run by two Christians, receives high marks for its innovative approach. For example, a volunteer family from the outside is assigned to every prisoner. A striking feature of this prison is the torture chamber. In that block only one cell is used. In that cell hangs a crucifix that was hand carved by the inmates. When asked about the crucifix in the torture chamber, inmates say that Jesus is doing time in their place.[1]

The inmates at Humaita realize that the only road to true freedom is through the cross. Jesus took on our sin and died in our place, taking the punishment and torture that were due us. Because He did that, He and He alone could claim to be the only way to the Father. His actions demonstrated that He was qualified to make this claim. When Jesus declared that He was the Way, the Truth, and the Life, He was making more than a theological statement. He was declaring to all that He could and would make a path for us to follow that would lead to the Father.

The inmates at Humaita also know that Jesus means a second opportunity at life for them. Because of God's grace that was demonstrated to them, these inmates have the opportunity to be changed. The change they are experiencing isn't external, social reform but inner change that can be accomplished only by the Holy Spirit, who lives and works inside them.

God wants to change or transform all of us into His image—what we were created to be. We can experience that change only through Jesus.

As you go through this day, think about what Jesus means to you. The inmates had a crucifix in the torture chamber to remind them that Jesus is the only way to the Father. What image symbolizes that reality in your life?

_____

With whom could you share this image? _____

_____

_____

_____

1. Charles Colson, "Making the World Safe for Religion," *Christianity Today*, 8 November 1993, 33.

DAY 4

In the math equations noted on page 105, the results will always be right when the formula is followed. The circumference of a circle can always be found by multiplying pi (π) by the diameter of the circle. It's just the way it works.

The passages included in the FAITH gospel presentation show that the path to salvation also follows an established plan. Paul used an important word in Romans 10:9-10. It can also be found in other passages in the FAITH gospel presentation. That word is *will*.

Quickly review the passages in the FAITH presentation (a complete outline is provided on pp. 10–11) and note the number of times you find the word will.

_____

Many things in life are uncertain. Many of our daily decisions are educated guesses. Even a doctor would have to admit that the diagnosis he gives a patient is usually an educated guess, based on the symptoms of our illness. Human beings just can't be sure about a lot of things.

The Bible doesn't say that if we confess Jesus as Lord and believe that God raised Him from the dead, we will most likely be saved. Nor does it say that there is a high probability that we will be saved. The Bible clearly states that we will be saved. If God promises something, we can believe it will happen.

Salvation is a sure thing. When something is a sure thing, we can build our lives on that reality. We would be foolish to build our entire lives on a guess or probability. The wills in the FAITH presentation indicate we can know for sure that we have salvation. That's good news!

As you go through this day, consider the wills—God's promises—in the gospel. List ways you can be sure of your salvation.

_____

_____

_____

_____

How does your assurance of salvation help you face today's challenges?

_____

_____

_____

_____

Thank God for providing a sure salvation.

DAY 5

As Dr. Rainer and his team interviewed lost people across America, they discovered a group of people who are resistant to the gospel. This resistant group, also called U4s, is not antagonistic, but they don't believe Christianity is true. Many believe in some kind of afterlife, but they don't generally believe in heaven or hell. Most, but not all, believe in some type of god, but they are unable to clearly define their belief. Even those interviewed who claimed they do not believe in God's existence, however, were open to the possibility.

Interestingly, most of this group respects the Bible. They may not believe it, but they are at least open to reading it. Some of those interviewed even read it every day. This discovery implies that a home Bible study may be an effective tool for reaching this group in our society.

Many U4s have one thing in common: they have had a bad experience in church or with churchgoing individuals. In many cases they felt condemned instead of loved. For example, Erik of Washington state associates church with several bad girlfriends: "Some of my worst experiences have been with ex-girlfriends who were religious. One once gave me an ultimatum: go to church or get lost. I couldn't believe that. She condemned me for not attending church services."[1] Obviously, we don't know all the details of this situation, but we know Erik has a lot of hurt from the way he perceived a church attender had treated him.

In the research conducted, 21 percent of the unchurched were found to be resistant or U4s. Dr. Rainer offered the following suggestions for sharing with a resistant unchurched person.

1. Don't be intimidated by the multiple arguments against Christianity a U4 may present. Depend on the Holy Spirit for strength and power.
2. Remember that most U4s are confused and searching. They may appear to be confident, but that confidence is usually a mask for their hurts and insecurities.
3. Remember that the culture faced by the early church, like our culture today, was secular, pluralistic, and ready to argue. However, the church saw some of its greatest advancements in that context.[2]

A surprise about resistant lost people is that 62 percent of those interviewed indicated they would be somewhat likely to attend a church if invited.[3]

Ask God to give you boldness and persistence in relating to those who are confused or initially resistant to the gospel.

1. Thom S. Rainer, *The Unchurched Next Door* (Grand Rapids, MI: Zondervan, 2003), 110.
2. Ibid., 112–13.
3. Ibid, 267.

SESSION

H IS FOR *HEAVEN*

SESSION GOALS

You will—
- examine scriptural pictures of heaven;
- identify ways heaven can be experienced on earth;
- present evidence for a literal heaven and hell;
- learn ways to transition to the Invitation portion of the FAITH gospel presentation.

What happens if a person is willing to repent of their sins and confess Christ?

H Is for *Heaven*

Heaven is a place where we will live with God forever.

"If I go away and prepare a place for you, I will come back and receive you to Myself, so that where I am you may be also."
John 14:3

Eternal life begins now with Jesus.
"I have come that they may have life and have it in abundance."
John 10:10

H can also stand for *how*.
How can a person have God's forgiveness, eternal life, and heaven?
By trusting Jesus as your Savior and Lord.

We began session 2 by thinking about our hometowns. There is no place like home. The water tastes better. The sun is brighter. The bed is more comfortable. For anyone who has been away for a while, there is nothing quite like the feeling of making that last turn and seeing home through the windshield. Being greeted by your family and being served your favorite meal add to the experience.

As great as our home may be, nothing compares to the home we will have in heaven. John tried to describe heaven in Revelation, but even that description falls short of what it will really be like. The last letter in the FAITH presentation is H, which stands for *heaven*. During this session we will unwrap God's promise of heaven and explore what it means for us today.

LOOKING FORWARD

One of the most meaningful and exciting doctrines of our faith is that God, who resides in heaven, invites the redeemed to live _____ in His _____. Heaven is the epitome of _____, _____, and _____. It is best understood as the place where God's _____ _____ dwells. Verses like John 3:16; Ephesians 2:1-10; 1 Peter 1:3-9; and Revelation 21:1-6 point to heaven.

At this point in the gospel presentation, we use John 14:3 to highlight the hope Christ gives us for enjoying heaven for eternity.

H Is for *Heaven*

Heaven is a place where we will live with God forever.
"If I go away and prepare a place for you, I will come back and receive you to Myself, so that where I am you may be also."
John 14:3

People have all sorts of ideas about what waits for us in heaven and what heaven is like. Not all of the ideas reflect the way Scripture describes heaven. Here is a partial list of things you may have heard someone say about heaven that are *not* taught in Scripture:

- Heaven is not a real or literal place.
- When people die and go to heaven, they become angels.
- All people will go to heaven when they die.
- Heaven is a paradise existence here on earth achieved by only a few persons.
- Before people can get into heaven, they must wait in a place called purgatory to be purged of their sins.
- Heaven is a place of sensual pleasure.

We could add more misconceptions to this list. The point is that not everyone with whom we dialogue about spiritual things will have the same concept of heaven that we do. As a matter of fact, some younger people may not have thought of heaven much because, in their perspective, heaven is a long way off. Recent surveys indicate that most people believe in heaven of some type and expect to go there when they die.

While Jesus was painfully enduring the cross, He declared to the crucified thief who repented and believed, "I assure you: Today you will be with Me in paradise" (Luke 23:43). Jesus referred to heaven as paradise. The Septuagint (a Greek translation of the Old Testament) calls the garden of Eden, mentioned in Genesis 2:8, the garden of paradise.[1] Before sin entered the world, the garden was a place where man and woman resided in a state of innocence. There they enjoyed their Maker's presence and experienced supreme happiness.

Jesus' use of the term *paradise* therefore conveys the idea of enjoying the _____ of our Creator. Other Scriptures add to this understanding:
- Heaven is a literal _____ (see John 14:2-3).
- Heaven is God's _____ place (see Matt. 6:9).
- Heaven is where _____ lives in bodily form (see Acts 7:55-56).
- Heaven is _____ (see 2 Cor. 5:1).
- Heavenly life is an eternal time of _____, _____, and _____ with God (see Matt. 26:29).
- Heaven is the place of God's throne and eternal _____ (see Rev. 22:3).
- Heaven is the future home of _____ (see 2 Cor. 5:1-2).
- Presently, all who have died in the _____ are there (see 2 Cor. 5:8).
- Heaven (the kingdom of God) is without the presence of _____ (see Gal. 5:19-21).
- Multitudes of _____ are in heaven praising God and attending Him (see Rev. 5:11).
- No _____ is in heaven (see Rev. 22:5).
- _____, _____, and _____ are not known in heaven (see Rev. 21:4).
- Heaven is the place where a believer's _____ is kept with care until the revelation of the Messiah (see 1 Pet. 1:4).

How would you describe heaven to a friend? _____

_____

_____

To what benefits of heaven are you most looking forward? _____

_____

THE REALITY OF HELL

To know what hell is, picture the opposites of the qualities of heaven listed above, except for the first one. Hell is not a figure of speech. Like heaven, it is a _____ _____. Jesus treated it as such (see Luke 16:19-24). The portraits of hell that we find in Scripture are not pretty. It is compared to a city dump (see 2 Kings 23:10) and is described as a place of constant _____ (see Mark 9:45) and _____, where worms constantly gnaw on whatever they can find (see Isa. 66:24). This is where those who reject God's gift of salvation will spend eternity—away from God's _____, _____, and _____.

We can be grateful that God has made forgiveness available so that those who accept His offer will never experience the ugliness and horror of hell.

ENJOYING A BIT OF HEAVEN NOW

Did you realize that when you asked Jesus to be your Savior, He gave you the capacity to have a life that is complete, full, and lived to its greatest potential? You were created to live in complete _____ with God and to enjoy being His most prized _____. The verse we use at this point in the FAITH gospel presentation clearly expresses the truth of heaven here—full, complete, abundant life.

Eternal life begins now with Jesus.
"I have come that they may have life and have it in abundance."
John 10:10

What does *abundant* mean? In this verse the Greek word for *abundant* "denotes the superabundance of the life Christ brings."[2] One dictionary indicates that the word *abundant* means "present in great quantity; more than adequate; well supplied; abounding; richly supplied."[3] These definitions indicate that abundant life is _____, _____, and lived to its highest _____ and beyond our _____.

Abundant life does not mean that you will never have sorrows, crises, disappointments, or defeats. It means that you will have the God who created you to personally nurture and direct your life. An abundant life is living a life directed by _____.

While abundant life also refers to our future in heaven, abundant life with _____ begins on earth _____. Various Scriptures highlight the quality of life that is available to us as Christians (see Rom. 8:12-17,26-30; Gal. 2:20; 3:26-27; 5:22-25; Eph. 1:9-14). Paul stated that spiritual life begins when a person accepts Jesus as Savior and is freed from the eternal consequences of rebellion against God: "If anyone is in Christ, there is a new creation; old things have passed away, and look, new things have come" (2 Cor. 5:17).

Many benefits result from living in a right relationship with God. Here are a few of them.

- Because of Christ's redeeming actions, we have been set _____ and are no longer condemned (see Rom. 8:1-2).
- We are made _____ of God and are thus able to share in His _____ (see Rom. 8:17).
- The Holy Spirit bears _____ in a believer's life (see Gal. 5:22-25).
- The Holy Spirit is the _____ of a believer's participation in heaven (see 2 Cor. 5:5).
- We are made new _____ and are reconciled to God (see 2 Cor. 5:17-18).

- We are made _____ in Christ and are brought close to Him (see Eph. 2:4-13).
- We can grow in a _____ with Christ and can know His power and fellowship (see Phil. 2:10).
- We have _____ (see Heb. 6:17-20).

When sharing with another person, you may want to characterize salvation as receiving a bit of heaven here on earth. You may want to use your evangelistic story, briefly sharing from your personal experience ways your life has changed and ways you have tasted heaven. Help people understand that Christianity isn't about simply avoiding hell but that it is about being the _____ _____ God created us to be. Certainly, that includes being with Him for eternity, but it also includes living a life of purpose and meaning here on earth.

HOW? MAKING THE TRANSITION

By this point in the gospel presentation, a person may want to know how he or she can have forgiveness and heaven. The letter *H* can also stand for *how*—how God took the _____ to save us through the death of His Son, Jesus, and how a person can have God's _____ and _____ _____ in heaven. By asking the how question—

> **How can a person have God's forgiveness, eternal life, and heaven?**

—you verbalize what the person is most likely thinking, opening the door for more dialogue.

You may want to ask if the person has questions or if what you have shared makes sense to them. Remember, you are about to ask someone if they want to make a decision for Christ. You want to give them time to process what you have shared and to make sure they fully understand the gospel message. Be sensitive to the Holy Spirit at this point. Some will be ready to make this decision, while others will need more time. Only the Holy Spirit can help you know what steps to take in each situation.

Explaining how a person can receive God's forgiveness and heaven sets the stage for the most important question of the visit:

> **Understanding what we have shared, would you like to receive this forgiveness by trusting in Christ as your personal Savior and Lord?**

With this question the conversation moves into the _____—when someone has the opportunity to receive personally the truth you have shared. Session 9 will explain how to make the transition into *how*, how to use *A Step of Faith* leaflet, and how to help a person make a decision for Christ.

AN OPPORTUNITY FOR CONTINUED DIALOGUE

The reality of _____ and _____
You may encounter a person who does not believe that a heaven or hell exists. You may even encounter some people who believe there is a heaven but not a hell. Obviously, as the passages we examined illustrate, the Bible clearly teaches that there are a literal heaven and a literal hell.

If the person with whom you are dialoguing believes there is a heaven but no hell, probe to learn the reason. You may want to point out that all creation points to the necessity of opposites. Hot and cold, big and small, light and dark, good and bad are all examples of things that demand that the other exists. How could you explain light without also explaining dark? It should be noted that these items in and of themselves are equals. Hot and cold are both of value and have a place in creation.

Both heaven and hell also have a place in creation. The reality of judgment demands that there be a place available for those who have a _____ sentence passed on them. Point out that it would be pointless for earthly governments to have courts and trials without having a means of punishing someone who was found guilty of a crime.

If the individual doesn't believe in any afterlife, ask what he or she believes. Ask probing questions to discover what they believe about the purpose of living and whether they believe history is heading in any particular direction. The Bible indicates that creation has _____ (see Jer. 29:11; Ps. 139:13-16) and is headed somewhere (see Matt. 13:37-43; 24:4-14).

GETTING PERSONAL

The thought of a better place should be a source of _____ to _____ _____ every day of our lives, just as it made a difference in the lives of the great leaders mentioned in the Bible. The writer of Hebrews helps us understand these leaders' motives in life: "These all died in faith without having received the promises, but they saw them from a distance, greeted them, and confessed that they were foreigners and temporary residents on the earth. Now those who say such things make it clear that they are seeking a homeland. If they had been remembering that land they came from, they would have had opportunity to return. But they now aspire to a better land—a heavenly one. Therefore God is not ashamed to be called their God, for He has prepared a city for them" (Heb. 11:13-16).

In what ways does the promise of heaven encourage you in your spiritual walk?

_____

_____

How can it help you endure hardships? _____

_____

_____

1. Adam Clarke, *Bible Commentary* [cited 8 July 2007]. Available from the Internet: *www.godrules.net/library/ clarke/clarkeluk23*.
2. Geoffrey W. Bromley, *Theological Dictionary of the New Testament*, ed. Gerhard Kittell and Gerhard Griedrich, trans. Geoffrey W. Bromley (Grand Rapids, MI: William B. Eerdmans Publishing Co., 1985), 829.
3. Stuart Berg Flexner, ed., *The Random House Unabridged Dictionary*, 2nd ed. (New York: Random House, Inc., 1993), 9.

MY FAITH CONNECTIONS

Visitation Summary

Attempts _____
Completed visits _____
Key Question asked _____

Record a synopsis of your team's visits. Include actions you may need to take on needs discovered. Whom should you tell about these needs? Prayer partners? Sunday School teacher? Minister?

_____

_____

_____

_____

_____

Life-Witness Summary

Key Question asked _____

_____

_____

_____

_____

My Journey This Week

What has God taught you this week? Record insights you have gained about God and yourself.

_____

_____

_____

_____

To-Do List

☐ Read session 8
☐ Completed "My FAITH Journey":
  ☐ Day 1
  ☐ Day 2
  ☐ Day 3
  ☐ Day 4
  ☐ Day 5

☐ **Contacted prayer partners**
☐ **Memorized "Invitation" section of FAITH presentation**
☐ **Reviewed "F Is for *Forgiveness*," "A Is for *Available*," "I Is for *Impossible*," "T Is for *Turn*," and "H Is for *Heaven*" sections of FAITH presentation**
☐ **Initiated spiritual dialogue with one person**
☐ _____
☐ _____
☐ _____
☐ _____
☐ _____
☐ _____

Prayer List

Lost people for whom you are praying:
☐ _____
☐ _____
☐ _____
☐ _____
☐ _____
☐ _____
☐ _____
☐ _____
☐ _____

Others needing prayer:
☐ _____
☐ _____
☐ _____
☐ _____
☐ _____
☐ _____
☐ _____
☐ _____

DAY 1

This week you learned that H is for *heaven*, completing your study of all five letters in the FAITH gospel presentation. Today let's build on what you have learned by preparing to examine the next step in the outline, the Invitation.

Imagine pulling into a new-car dealership and seeing the car of your dreams. It's in the color you have always wanted and has all the extra features you would choose. It seems to be sitting there waiting for you. As you stare at the car, a man approaches you. Together you talk about the car's capabilities and features. You are so excited you can hardly stand it. You are ready to drive the car off the lot.

You ask the man if he has seen a salesperson. He replies that he is a salesperson. He thanks you for letting him tell you about the car and lets you know you are more than welcome to come by anytime and look at this car. Then he turns and walks away to the office area, leaving you standing in the lot.

That scenario would be preposterous. If all we do is share Jesus with others and never give them the opportunity to accept Christ, we are like the car salesperson who turned and walked away. Unfortunately, many well-intentioned people tell others how Jesus has made a difference in their lives; yet they never explain how their friends can make that same discovery. We have a responsibility to give them that opportunity. Failing to do so is cruel and disobedient.

In the next session we will discover ways to help someone make a decision for Christ. The FAITH gospel presentation concludes with a three-part section called the Invitation. Memorize this section just as you have memorized the letters F-A-I-T-H. Then you will have memorized all of the FAITH gospel presentation. The three parts are:

Inquire
Understanding what we have shared, would you like to receive this forgiveness by trusting in Christ as your personal Savior and Lord?

Invite

Insure

As you learn the Invitation, also review this process for using A *Step of Faith* leaflet in that dialogue. We will look at it in detail in the next session.

1. As you make transition by asking *how* (under *Heaven*), show A *Step of Faith*.
2. Discuss the picture; identify with one of the people; and talk about the modern clothing, the hammers, and the spikes in their hands. Talk about our sin putting Jesus on the cross.
3. Turn to panel 2 for a review of *Forgiveness, Available,* and *Impossible*.
4. Refer to panel 3 for a review of *Turn*. As you turn to panel 4, say something like "Just as I am turning this page, we need to turn from sin and self and turn to Someone, Jesus."
5. Once again, briefly review H is for *heaven* on panel 4, which leads to the commitment question you are learning this week:

Understanding what we have shared, would you like to receive this forgiveness by trusting in Christ as your personal Savior and Lord?

If the person does not want to make a commitment to Christ at this time, leave the leaflet behind. All of the information that was shared is included in this leaflet. If he responds that he wants to accept Christ, guide him to pray a prayer that reflects the decision of his heart.

6. After the person prays to receive Christ, move to panel 6, "Commitment Card." Fill in each blank, explaining to the new believer what each point represents.

7. Discuss meeting for a Bible study class and answer any questions the individual has about church.

8. In closing the visit, pray a thanksgiving prayer with the new believer. Encourage the new believer to pray, expressing thanks, and also pray about any needs that may have arisen during the visit.

9. Your FAITH team has the privilege of returning next week to begin discipling your new Christian friend in his new faith.

DAY 2

James Black was a teacher of a Sunday School class for teenagers. One day he met a 14-year-old girl and invited her to Sunday School. She accepted his invitation. During one of the group's meetings one evening, members were asked to answer roll call by quoting a Scripture text. When it was the girl's turn, she could not respond. Touched by what he had witnessed, Black spoke about the importance of answering God's roll call and about how sad it would be if someone's name were not included when the book of life was read. He wanted to sing a song that would sum up what he was thinking and feeling, but he could find nothing on the spur of the moment that seemed adequate. While on his way home, Black continued to think about the experience and the need for a song that would communicate the importance of being on heaven's roll.

The thought crossed Black's mind that he should write such a song, but he dismissed it. When he reached home, his wife, noticing that he was preoccupied, questioned him. He made no reply. He simply sat thinking. Before the evening was over, he had written the words and the music for the song he had so desperately wanted earlier. We know this song as "When the Roll Is Called Up Yonder."[1]

As you go through this day, meditate on the first verse of this song. Reflect on the victory it reflects and on the fact that you will be a participant in this scene.

> When the trumpet of the Lord shall sound and time shall be no more,
> And the morning breaks, eternal, bright, and fair,
> When the saved on earth shall gather over on the other shore,
> And the roll is called up yonder, I'll be there.[2]

1. William J. Reynolds, *Companion to Baptist Hymnal* (Nashville: Broadman Press, 1976), 242–43.
2. *The Baptist Hymnal* (Nashville: Convention Press, 1991), 516.

DAY 3

During session 8 we learned that there is more to the Christian life than avoiding hell. Peter encouraged his readers to "grow in the grace and knowledge of our Lord and Savior Jesus Christ" (2 Pet. 3:18). To grow up implies that we as Christians have something to do while we wait for heaven. Paul used the same image when he addressed the Corinthian believers, comparing them to a baby and directing them to put away childish things (see 1 Cor 3:1-3; 13:11). At the core of this idea is what it means to be saved.

In session 7 we briefly considered the meaning of salvation when we examined Romans 10:9-10 (see pp. 105–6). We can look at salvation from the perspective of what Jesus did and does, but we can also look at it from a human perspective. Our experience of salvation encompasses the past, present, and future. God's ongoing work in a believer's life after conversion relates to at least three areas:

1. The process of maturing in Christ (see Heb. 2:3; 1 Pet. 2:2)
2. Growing in Christ's service (see 1 Cor. 7:20-22)
3. Experiencing victory over sin through the power of the Holy Spirit (see Rom. 7–8)

Believers are living between what God has begun and what He is yet to complete (see Phil. 1:6; 2:12). We are in the process of becoming what God created us to be, both as individuals and as His people. This process of becoming produces the abundant life that Jesus announced in John 10:10: "I have come that they may have life and have it in abundance." The normal Christian life is characterized by spiritual growth, as opposed to simply existing until we get to heaven.

Think back over the past few weeks. Is there a certain area of your life that God has been working on? ☐ Yes ☐ No

How has He changed you in the past four weeks? _____

_____

_____

_____

How has the knowledge that God is doing something in your life helped you cope with difficulties?

_____

_____

_____

_____

Thank God for being involved in your life and for moving you toward what He created you to be.

DAY 4

No doubt, there are people around you who are living a hell on earth. They have little hope, and to them, life seems to get more complicated every day.

Identify one or two persons who would fit into this category.

_____

Review on pages 117–19 the characteristics of heaven with Jesus and eternal life that begins now. Record one or two characteristics that would speak directly to the person or persons you identified.

_____

_____

How would the characteristics you identified be of value to these persons? Why did you select the ones you did?

_____

_____

_____

_____

_____

How could you communicate these characteristics of heaven to the persons you identified? What images, illustrations, or Bible stories could you use to help them realize the truth of the characteristics you identified?

_____

_____

_____

_____

Ask God to give you an opportunity to share with the person or persons you identified. Thank Him in advance for the opportunity He will give you and for the right words He will place in your mouth.

DAY 5

Today we will look at the group of unchurched people identified by Dr. Rainer and his research team as U5s or antagonists.

Jerry called himself neutral toward the church, but he had definite opinions about Christian beliefs that were anything but neutral. For example, he viewed Jesus as a fictional character created to make people do the right thing. He had little tolerance for Christians who wanted to "impose their beliefs" on him.

Like most antagonists interviewed, Jerry had certain trigger points that pointed to a bad church experience. Most antagonists were unwilling to share about their church experiences, putting up an instant wall.[1]

Most of the antagonists encountered were educated and wealthy. Most had embraced the idea that religion is an insult to the rational. They had no room for God or anything else that could not be explained rationally. Ironically, most of the antagonistic, although the most educated unchurched group, are ignorant of the doctrines of Christianity. Unlike the other groups of unchurched people, this group indicated that they would not attend a church even if invited by a friend. Only 5 percent of those interviewed were classified as antagonists—by far the minority.[2]

Dr. Rainer suggests that when you talk with U5s, challenge them with a deeper cognitive approach. Various books could be used to equip you for such a conversation, including C. S. Lewis's *Mere Christianity*. (Lewis was a philosophical agnostic who became an evangelical Christian.) Helpful discipleship studies in this area are *When Worldviews Collide* by Ergun Caner and *The Ever-Loving Truth* by Voddie Baucham Jr.

The biggest issues you will most likely face in engaging antagonists are deep hurt and anger. If these emotions are expressed, remember that they are usually directed toward the hurt and not toward you. To reach U5s, you will need to develop long-term relationships with the persons and move them toward Christianity through intelligent, honest dialogue.

Pray for U5s, asking that God will soften their hearts and place persons in their lives who will be willing to invest in friendships with them in order to lead them to Christ.

1. Thom Rainer, *The Unchurched Next Door* (Grand Rapids, MI: Zondervan, 2003), 63–66.
2. Ibid., 79–100.

MY FAITH JOURNEY

SESSION

THE INVITATION

SESSION GOALS

You will—

- identify ways to transition to the Invitation portion of the FAITH gospel presentation;
- understand how to use *A Step of Faith* leaflet;
- learn how to invite a person to accept Christ without *A Step of Faith* leaflet.

Inquire
Understanding what we have shared, would you like to receive this forgiveness by trusting in Christ as your personal Savior and Lord?

Invite

Insure

Imagine you have just had the opportunity to share the FAITH gospel presentation for the first time. Your friend appears to be attentive to everything you have shared. His questions are good ones—for clarification—and you've been able to answer them. You are excited that you remembered all the Scripture passages and points in the FAITH outline. What do you do next? How do you help someone respond to what you have shared?

During this session we will examine ways to help someone respond to the gospel. We will learn how to introduce the idea of a _____ to the good news and how to use a _____ to help you invite a response. Then we'll suggest ideas for leading toward a response when you don't have the leaflet with you.

A LIFE-CHANGING DECISION

Think about the decision you are placing before the person with whom you have shared Christ. All kinds of things have occurred before this moment. Difficulties in life may have precipitated some hard questions about God's love and salvation. The person may be someone you have shared with for a long time or a complete stranger to you just 30 minutes before. Every situation is different. The one certainty, however, is the nature of the decision the person faces.

Salvation is a _____ _____. It changes who we are, what we do, and whom we associate with. It is about turning from the path we once walked and following Jesus. *Everything* has the potential of changing with this one decision. You called your conversion a life-changing experience when you shared your evangelistic story, and so it is. The decision is even more than deciding to believe certain things about Jesus and God; it is about placing _____ in Jesus and living a life that is worthy of His _____.

Therefore, this is not a decision to be taken lightly or without considering what it may mean later. We must give everyone an opportunity to consider, grasp, and respond to the gospel. How this happens will be different for each person.

LEADING TO A RESPONSE

In the previous session we discovered that *H* in the FAITH outline, in addition to denoting *heaven,* can also stand for *how.* This is the point in the dialogue in which you will begin to use A *Step of Faith* leaflet.

H can also stand for *how.*

**How can a person have God's forgiveness, eternal life, and heaven?
By trusting Jesus as your Savior and Lord.**

You may want to add a _____ _____ after asking, "How can a person have God's forgiveness, eternal life, and heaven?" For example,

"Is that something you would like to do?" or "Have you ever thought about making this kind of commitment?"

Then let the person _____. Ask _____ to help you know what to do next. If the person responds in a way that shows a lack of understanding about what you have shared, _____ about the issue(s) that appear to create difficulty. Allow _____ for him or her to think and talk about what you have shared. You may say something like "Receiving Christ as Savior is the greatest decision you can make. It is a life-changing decision and the right decision. Do you have a question about what we have been talking about?" Although your desire is to see individuals accept Christ as Savior, take care in leading someone to a genuine commitment. Do not _____ them or appear _____.

At times it may be necessary to _____ the conversation on another day. You might offer to meet over lunch for further dialogue or to reschedule another visit. Sometimes you may suggest joining some friends from your Sunday School class for relationship building and discussion.

As a witness, you don't know what the person is thinking and what God has been doing or is doing in his life. You also don't know the urgency of the situation. Life is uncertain, and tomorrow is not promised (see Jas. 4:13-15). At the same time, don't force anyone to do something he is not ready to do. The bottom line is that only _____ knows what tomorrow holds and how _____ you should be when leading a person to make a decision for Christ.

At this critical juncture, continue to depend on the _____ _____, listening to Him every step of the way as you share. He is the One who brings conviction of sin and leads to a response, using you in the process. If someone is open and willing, you can help him or her make a commitment to Jesus.

A STEP OF FAITH

A TOOL TO HELP SOMEONE TAKE A STEP OF FAITH

Pictures help us express our feelings or identify with an event or emotion. Because pictures have different meanings to different people, someone's response to or opinion about a picture is correct for him or her. In addition, a person's response to a picture usually reveals more about the one responding than about the subject of the picture.

A picture is the key feature of A *Step of Faith* leaflet. It is there to help people express personal _____ and _____ about _____. It should spur the spiritual dialogue on to a higher level.

Look at the front of A Step of Faith. *What do you think this picture represents? Why?*

_____

_____

_____

What do you think Jesus is saying to you personally through this picture?

_____

_____

What would you say to an unsaved person about this picture? _____

_____

_____

When using *A Step of Faith*, first introduce the person to the picture. Briefly call attention to _____ on the cross paying the price for our sins; to the different people and the contemporary clothing; to the wide range of _____ that are evident—deep remorse, grief, and shock. Call attention to the mallets (hammers) and spikes. The people in the illustration have been or are still holding mallets; it is as though they have been driving the spikes into Jesus' hands and feet.

F IS FOR **FORGIVENESS**

Everyone has sinned and needs God's forgiveness. His forgiveness is available in Jesus.

"All have sinned and fall short of the glory of God." Romans 3:23

"In Him we have redemption through His blood, the forgiveness of our trespasses, according to the riches of His grace." Ephesians 1:7

A IS FOR **AVAILABLE**

God's forgiveness is available to all, but it is not automatic.

"God loved the world in this way: He gave His One and Only Son, so that everyone who believes in Him will not perish but have eternal life." John 3:16

"Not everyone who says to Me, 'Lord, Lord!' will enter the kingdom of heaven." Matthew 7:21

I IS FOR **IMPOSSIBLE**

According to the Bible, it is impossible to get to heaven on our own.

"By grace you are saved through faith, and this is not from yourselves; it is God's gift." Ephesians 2:8

So how can a sinful person have eternal life and enter heaven?

2

T IS FOR **TURN**

If you were going down the road and someone asked you to turn, what would he or she be asking you to do?

CHANGE DIRECTION. GO A DIFFERENT WAY. REPENT.

"Unless you repent, you will all perish as well!" Luke 13:3

"I am the way, the truth, and the life. No one comes to the Father except through Me." John 14:6

"If you confess with your mouth, 'Jesus is Lord,' and believe in your heart that God raised Him from the dead, you will be saved. With the heart one believes, resulting in righteousness, and with the mouth one confesses, resulting in salvation." Romans 10:9-10

3

What an overwhelming realization: our sins made it necessary for Jesus to die. However, His death on the cross for our sins is the way we can have God's forgiveness and salvation.

Ask, "Whom do you think the people in this picture _____?" One obvious answer is that they represent people from different cultural/ethnic groups. A person could look at the picture and identify a friend, a neighbor, or an associate. You may ask, "Of the people in this picture, which one best represents ____?" This gives you an opportunity to understand what the person might think and feel.

You may want to share what you feel when you see this illustration. Be careful to let the other person share more than you share. It is not about you. It is about the individual gaining an image of the _____ of Christ's death and the _____ He expressed in that death.

After the person has responded to the illustration, begin to briefly review the _____ _____, using panels 2–4 of A Step of Faith. Ask whether the person has any questions about F (Forgiveness), A (Available), or I (Impossible) from your earlier discussion. Clarify any Scriptures as needed.

The important action of turning is described on panel 3. At this point, refer to this part of A Step of Faith for a review of the letter T (turn). Allow the question to help you clarify the meaning of _____ to Christ and so changing the total _____ of one's life. As you turn from panel 3 to panel 4, say something like "Just as I am turning this page, we need to turn from sin and self and turn to Someone—Jesus."

Reviewing panel 4 and the meanings of heaven, including that H also stands for how, may give you the joy and opportunity of leading someone to make a personal _____ to Christ. By asking the how question (also on their leaflet)— "How can a person have God's forgiveness, eternal life, and heaven?"—you may be verbalizing what the person is most likely thinking, opening the door for more dialogue. Continue to rely on the Holy Spirit as you help the person discover that forgiveness is possible by trusting Jesus as Savior and Lord. What a holy moment!

As is natural and comfortable for you, you may want to emphasize that each finger on your hand could stand for a letter in the FAITH gospel presentation. Say, "In my hand I have the leaflet with the picture we just talked about." Extend your hand with the leaflet in it. "I would like to give you this leaflet. For you to have this leaflet, you must reach out and take it from me. In the same way, God is offering you forgiveness, but just as you take this leaflet, you have to accept His forgiveness for it to be yours."

H IS FOR **HEAVEN**

Heaven is a place where we will live with God forever.

"If I go away and prepare a place for you,
I will come back and receive you to Myself,
so that where I am you may be also."
John 14:3

Eternal life begins now with Jesus.

"I have come that they may have life
and have it in abundance."
John 10:10

H CAN ALSO STAND FOR **HOW.**

How can a person have God's forgiveness, eternal life, and heaven?

By trusting Jesus as personal Savior and Lord.

Dear God, I know that You love me.
I confess my sin and need of salvation.
I believe that Jesus died on the cross
for my sins and arose from the grave.

I turn away from my sin and place my
faith in Jesus as my Savior and Lord.
I want to follow You with my life.
Amen.

4

Do what is most comfortable for you and for the person with whom you are sharing. The important thing is to support, not detract from, the message. Your main goal is to ask the _____ _____ in the FAITH gospel presentation, thus giving someone the opportunity to accept Jesus as Savior and Lord. Remember, you don't want to present what someone needs in his life without offering an opportunity to accept God's gracious gift of forgiveness.

> **Inquire**
> **Understanding what we have shared, would you like to receive this forgiveness by trusting in Christ as your personal Savior and Lord?**
>
> *A person could respond to this question in many ways. List some of the responses you have heard during FAITH training.*

_____

_____

_____

The most obvious answers are yes or no. However, some people may tell you they have already made this decision (ask them to tell you about it), that they need some time to think about it, that they want to talk it over with their parents or spouse, or that they cannot do this today. Be sensitive to the Holy Spirit at this point. Trust Him to tell you how to proceed if the answer is something other than a clear yes.

LEADING SOMEONE TO ASK GOD FOR FORGIVENESS

By inviting someone to accept Christ, you have the opportunity both to _____ the good news and to _____ a person to _____ to receive Christ. If a person wants to pray this life-changing prayer, you may be able to help him or her express this commitment.

Leading someone to pray a _____ of _____ becomes a meaningful expression of that person's decision to accept God's offer of forgiveness and salvation and to begin following Christ. Some people may be reluctant because they have never prayed out loud before. Assure them that God does not want or expect eloquent words or particular phrases in a prayer. God wants us to be honest with Him.

Having *A Step of Faith* leaflet may be invaluable to this person. At this point you can call attention to the salvation prayer printed on panel 4. The exact words are

> *Dear God, I know that You love me. I confess my sin and need of salvation. I believe that Jesus died on the cross for my sins and arose from the grave.*
>
> *I turn away from my sin and place my faith in Jesus as my Savior and Lord. I want to follow You with my life. Amen.*

not a magic formula, but a printed prayer can be a great deal of help, especially if you are dialoguing with someone who has little religious background.

You may want to read the printed prayer aloud. Ask something like "Does this prayer reflect what you _____ to do?" Indicate that the person can pray his own prayer or use the one in the leaflet to commit his life to Christ. State, "If you want to make this commitment, _____ _____ what you are thinking and what you want to do. Or use this printed prayer as a guide." Then wait for a response, again being extremely sensitive to the Holy Spirit.

If the person asks for God's forgiveness, _____ with him. _____ him and _____ what he has just done. Point to Romans 10:9 (on panel 3), highlighting the promise that God will save those who put their trust in Jesus (we will examine this more in the next session) and acknowledging how He saved you when you put your trust in Him.

After the person has prayed, use A Step of Faith again. The Commitment Card (panel 6) allows you to walk the person through _____ _____ of commitments. In general, lead the person to check the box adjacent to the first statement and to write the _____ and _____ of his or her decision for Christ. Because this leaflet will remain with the person, A Step of Faith can be a meaningful memento of the decision.

Move to the next statement on the Commitment Card (panel 6) about taking _____ _____ of faith and obedience. Indicate that the church, as the body of Christ, provides the support and the opportunities to begin to grow in Christ.

Highlight the benefits of a caring _____ _____ _____ as you move to the final statement. Invite the person to allow you to enroll him or her in a class. Emphasize that enrolling in a class does not mean the person is joining your church. Ask the person to check the statement if he or she is willing to be enrolled in a Sunday School class.

Although some of this information will be explained more in your follow-up visit, briefly overview the way your church receives new members. Help the person understand what will happen when she is presented to the church. For example: "Mrs. Jones, our pastor, Jim Smith, will introduce you to the church family. He wants to know who you are, and he wants others in our church to know and support you. He will pray for you and for the others who are standing. Some of us will be by your side since we are all in the same Sunday School class. It's a special time in our church that will help you feel welcome."

COMMITMENT CARD

Name _____

Address _____

_____

_____

Phone _____

Birth date _____

I commit to …

☐ **Accept Jesus as my Savior and Lord.**

Date and place of my decision:

Date _____

Place _____

☐ **Take the next steps in following Jesus.**

☐ **Join a Bible-study group.**

6

PEOPLE WHO MADE THE VISIT

_____

_____

_____

FOLLOW-UP VISIT

_____

NOTES

_____

_____

_____

_____

_____

_____

_____

_____

_____

_____

_____

_____

_____

7

MY COMMITMENT

I accept Jesus as my Savior and Lord.

Date _____

Place _____

Friend _____

NEXT STEPS
IN FOLLOWING JESUS

Baptism: standing for God

Prayer: talking with God

Bible study: discovering God's will

Devotional life: experiencing God

Church with other believers: spending time with God's people

Sharing Jesus with others: talking about what God has done for you through Jesus

5

Panel 7, the reverse side of the Commitment Card, reveals another use of _A Step of Faith:_ to record _____ about the person's decision(s). Gather as much information as you can so that appropriate follow-up steps can be taken. Tear off the Commitment Card at the perforation and return it to the appropriate FAITH leader at your church. After the visit, record when the team's follow-up visit should be made.

Next, call attention to "_____ _____in Following Jesus" on panel 5. Explain that _disciple_ is another name for a follower of Jesus. Explain that being a part of Sunday School or a small group can help them grow in their spiritual journey. Highlight baptism, explaining that you would like to visit at a later date to address that subject.

Point out the lines available on panel 5 for the new believer to record information about her decision for Christ. State that you will leave the remainder of the leaflet with the person as a _____ of this life-changing decision.

In closing the visit, pray a prayer of _____ with the new believer. Encourage the person to pray, expressing thanks to God. If any needs have been expressed during the visit, lift those needs to God at this time as well. Leave the remainder of the leaflet with the new believer.

LEADING TO A DECISION WITHOUT A LEAFLET

Suppose that you find an opportunity to ask the Key Question in a daily-life encounter. The person gives a works response and permission for you to share how the Bible answers this question. You move through the FAITH gospel presentation, and the person seems to be under conviction by the Holy Spirit.

You don't have a copy of A Step of Faith. *What should you do?* _____

_____

_____

_____

_____

_____

_____

Sometimes you won't have *A Step of FAITH* leaflet with you when have an opportunity to lead someone to a decision for Christ. Here are some steps you can take to lead the person to invite Jesus into their heart.

First, review the _____ subpoint in the letter *H* by saying something like the following.

> *[Person's name], you may be asking yourself,* How can a person have God's forgiveness, eternal life, and heaven? *We've said that H stands for heaven; it can also stand for how. (Extend your hand.)*
>
> *[Person's name], look at your hand. Remember how we just spelled out meanings of the word FAITH on our hands?*
>
> *[Person's name], if you turn from your own way of trying to make life work and reach out with your own hand of faith to Jesus, you can find this same forgiveness, eternal life, and heaven.*
>
> *You can know for certain that you are on the right road, and you can receive God's forgiveness, eternal life, and heaven. Remember what we said earlier: "If you confess with your mouth, 'Jesus is Lord,' and believe in your heart that God raised Him from the dead, you will be saved."*
>
> *[Person's name], do you understand what we've shared? If so, would you like to receive this forgiveness by trusting in Christ as your personal Savior and Lord?*

If the person says yes, lead him to pray a simple prayer for salvation. One of the most important concepts in receiving salvation is to turn from sin to trust Christ only. Help the person understand the necessity of realizing that he is a sinner, of asking God for _____, of repenting from his _____, and of acknowledging Jesus' death and resurrection as the only way to be saved. The brief prayer should reflect these understandings.

Take time this week to make sure you are ready to help a person make a decision for Christ. You may want to create a file for your PDA; prepare a laminated card with the salvation prayer; or stock up on A Step of Faith leaflets, placing one in your purse, daily planner, Bible, wallet, or another item you always carry.

INSURE

As you close your visit, help the new believer be sure of what he or she has just done. You can do several things to help.

- Review the _____ _____ in the FAITH outline, highlighting the promises included in each passage.
- Share your _____.
- Point to the _____ _____ panel in *A Step of Faith* leaflet, emphasizing the importance of documenting and remembering the date of this meaningful personal decision.
- Ask the individual to explain in his own words the _____ just made.

What else could you do to help a new believer be confident of his or her decision?

_____

_____

_____

_____

_____

By giving some attention to assurance, you may prevent the new believer from falling into the doubt trap.

Finally, _____ a prayer of thanksgiving with the new Christian, remembering to pray for any needs discovered during the visit and asking God to help the person learn more about Him. Encourage him to _____ the leaflet. Offer to _____ _____ in the next few days to make arrangements for Sunday and to offer Bible study materials.

MY FAITH CONNECTIONS

Visitation Summary

Attempts _____
Completed visits _____
Key Question asked _____

Record a synopsis of your team's visits. Include actions you may need to take on needs discovered. Whom should you tell about these needs? Prayer partners? Sunday School teacher? Minister?

_____

_____

_____

_____

Life-Witness Summary

Key Question asked _____

_____

_____

_____

_____

My Journey This Week

What has God taught you this week? Record insights you have gained about God and yourself.

_____

_____

_____

_____

To-Do List

☐ Read session 9
☐ Completed "My Faith Journey":
  ☐ Day 1
  ☐ Day 2
  ☐ Day 3
  ☐ Day 4
  ☐ Day 5

☐ Contacted prayer partners
☐ Reviewed FAITH presentation
☐ Wrote baptism testimony
☐ Initiated spiritual dialogue
  with one person
☐ _____
☐ _____
☐ _____
☐ _____
☐ _____

Prayer List

Lost people for whom you are praying.
☐ _____
☐ _____
☐ _____
☐ _____
☐ _____
☐ _____
☐ _____
☐ _____
☐ _____
☐ _____
☐ _____
☐ _____

Others needing prayer:
☐ _____
☐ _____
☐ _____
☐ _____
☐ _____
☐ _____
☐ _____
☐ _____
☐ _____
☐ _____

DAY 1

MY FAITH JOURNEY

"My FAITH Journey" assignments for sessions 4–8 examined research done by Dr. Thom Rainer about the unchurched in the United States. Rainer and his research team identified five categories of unchurched people—the highly receptive, the receptive, the neutral, the resistant, and the antagonist. One surprising finding of the research was that 80 percent of the unchurched interviewed said they would attend church with someone if they were invited.

As important as inviting someone to church may be, if that is all we do, we fail to do the best thing for the person. There is a difference between inviting someone to church and inviting someone to accept Jesus. Here are a few differences (you may want to add your own ideas):

Invite to Church	*Invite to Jesus*
Relate to other humans	Relate to God
Make a difference on earth	Make a difference on earth and in heaven
Do the right thing	Become righteous
Invite to an imperfect place	Invite to the perfect place (heaven)

Inviting a person to Jesus is the ultimate invitation we could deliver to anyone. We hope you have been cultivating friendships with unchurched people over the past weeks.

Are there people you have invited to church but have not invited to Jesus?
☐ Yes   ☐ No

Ask God to help you invite at least one person to Jesus this week.

DAY 2

The story of Philip is a fascinating one (see Acts 8:26-39). While having some success preaching to the Samaritans, Philip was told by an angel of the Lord to go to Gaza. The road from Jerusalem was dangerous and lacked the promise of the Samaritan villages. There would be little hope of finding a stranger to share Jesus with on this road, but Philip did what he was asked to do.

If you had been Philip, would you have heard God's message?   ☐ Yes ☐ No

Would you have paid attention?   ☐ Yes ☐ No

Would you have discredited or ignored what the angel was saying? ☐ Yes ☐ No

Would you have left success to take the risk of obedience?   ☐ Yes ☐ No

Philip responded by taking the desert road. There he encountered an Ethiopian government official and had the opportunity to share with him about Christ.

During FAITH training you have been encouraged to be sensitive to the Holy Spirit when dialoguing with another person. Every contact, every visit, every opportunity to share with another person is different. As you talk to two persons, one may completely tune out what you are saying, while the other desperately hangs on to every word. We must pay attention to the Holy Spirit to understand how to approach each situation.

In your daily life God may have been quietly telling you to approach a particular individual. You may have ignored God's promptings, hoping they would go away.

During the next 24 hours ask God to give you the courage to respond to His promptings. Ask God to place someone in your life who needs to hear the gospel. Be bold enough to ask God to identify that person to you. Then promise to pay attention to what He tells you to do.

DAY 3

God parted the waters for His people on two occasions. The first was at the Red Sea as the Egyptians pursued them (see Ex. 14). The second occurred a little more than 40 years later as Joshua led the Hebrews across the Jordan River into the promised land (see Josh. 3). After they entered the promised land, God told Joshua to select 12 men, one from each family grouping, to go back into the river bed and remove one stone each. They carried the stones to the campsite in Gilgal. Joshua also stacked 12 stones in the place where the priests had stood as the people crossed over. After the stones were set up in Gilgal, Joshua explained the importance of the stone display. This display would remind future generations of God's actions on behalf of His people (see Josh. 4:21-24). These stones were a physical reminder of a spiritual event.

When you think about the day you committed your life to Christ, you can probably identify some spiritual markers. It may be a date written in a specific Bible. It may be an entry in a journal or diary. Maybe a place, a song, a Bible verse, or another memorable item reminds you of that important decision. Whatever it is, it can have the same purpose as the stone memorial set up by Joshua.

We all need reminders of key days in our lives. None is more important than a reminder of our decision to follow Christ. Not every day feels like that first day after salvation, and we need to be reminded of it. These physical objects are God's gifts of assurance to us.

Think about the day you accepted Christ as your Savior. Remember as much as you can about it. If you can, visit the location or read a Bible verse that spoke to you on that day. Thank God for His salvation and the assurance that He has saved you.

DAY 4

There is nothing like being there when your favorite team wins. Watching the game on television may be easier and less expensive, but if you had a choice, you would be there. Painting your face to sit at home just doesn't compare to celebrating a victory in person with all the other face-painted fans.

In a way, when you are there, you become part of the event. The officials don't hear someone watching the game on television. You just know your team won because you stood to your feet and assisted the officials in making the right call!

As much fun as it may be to celebrate in the stands when your team wins, how much more fun it is to celebrate a new believer's salvation with him or her. Hearing others share about being there when a person accepts Christ is nice, but it doesn't compare to being there yourself and witnessing it firsthand. Like a fan at a ball game, you become part of the event. What some people will remember about their conversion day is you. Celebration is important because it serves as a reminder of the day salvation came to someone's life.

How could you celebrate a person's decision to follow Christ? _____

_____

_____

_____

_____

_____

_____

Scan Luke 15, looking for the celebrations described. When each item or person was found, there was a celebration. Ask God to help you celebrate your salvation and the salvation of others.

DAY 5

When people accept Jesus, they begin a new journey characterized by obedience to God. One simple act of obedience is baptism. While it is a picture of Jesus' death, burial, and resurrection, it is also a way to publicly declare a commitment to Christ. Many people use the act of baptism to share with their family and friends about their decision to follow Jesus. These friends and relatives are invited to witness this act, giving the new believer an opportunity to explain why he or she was baptized. It is a simple yet important step in any believer's life.

When you lead a person to Christ, you have the opportunity to help him or her take next step of following Jesus, including baptism. In the next session we will discover some tools that will help you communicate the importance of baptism. One tool is a testimony about your own baptism. Such a testimony could have three short parts. Perhaps you can remember the parts with these words: *after, next,* and *although*. The following example uses this format.

- *After* I prayed and trusted Jesus only as my Savior, I was thankful that He was not ashamed of me and had died for me. I was not ashamed to obey and follow Jesus in scriptural baptism.
- *Next,* I was baptized by a minister in the Belle Oaks Church.
- *Although* I knew baptism did not save me, I understood that it symbolized what had happened—dying to my sins, burying my former rebellious life, and being raised to a new life in following Jesus.

Write a testimony about your baptism, using the words identified.

After: _____

_____

_____

_____

Next: _____

_____

_____

_____

Although: _____

_____

_____

_____

Pray that in your follow-up visit this week and at other times, God will use you to lend support to your new believer-friend who is starting the journey of faith.

MY FAITH JOURNEY

SESSION

THEY ACCEPTED JESUS; NOW WHAT?

SESSION GOALS

You will—
- define your responsibility after leading a person to Jesus;
- be able to explain the importance of baptism;
- demonstrate how to use *Next Steps in Following Jesus* leaflet.

When people accept Jesus, they immediately receive the Holy Spirit, who lives inside them, teaches them spiritual truth, and helps them grow in the likeness of Christ. First John 2:27 describes the Holy Spirit's teaching role in a believer's life: "The anointing you received from Him remains in you, and you don't need anyone to teach you. Instead, His anointing teaches you about all things, and is true and is not a lie; just as it has taught you, remain in Him."

God has assigned the body of Christ, the church, a role in teaching believers as well, "for the training of the saints in the work of ministry, to build up the body of Christ, until we all reach unity in the faith and in the knowledge of God's Son, growing into a mature man with a stature measured by Christ's fullness" (Eph. 4:12-13). Too many times new believers who are born into the kingdom become spiritual orphans because the church fails to fulfill its responsibility to teach and disciple them.

When believers lead people to Christ, we are responsible for them as their _____ _____. Paul assumed this role in training Timothy, whom he considered his son in the ministry (see Phil. 2:22). Like a newborn baby, a new believer needs to learn how to walk and survive in this world. Some of the basics you can teach new believers include setting aside time alone with God, learning how to study the Bible and pray, using spiritual gifts for God's glory, and sharing Jesus with others. You may also recruit some to be prayer partners or team members for the next semester of FAITH training.

Eventually, new Christians will move beyond needing us for the basics, and we will become their encouragers and supporters. In the Great Commission Jesus told us to make _____, not just converts (see Matt. 28:19-20). The ultimate goal for a person who comes to Christ is to grow up in the Lord and become a spiritual _____, leading others to Christ and teaching them how to live. Continuing the process is what being a disciple is all about.

As you cultivate relationships, visit the lost, and witness, keep in mind that when someone experiences spiritual birth, your work is not over. In most cases your work is just beginning.

DEFINING MOMENTS

In our lives there are usually only a handful of defining moments. Though few, these experiences are vivid to us, as if they happened just yesterday. In our minds we have relived these moments many times. These experiences define who we are as individuals.

List some defining moments in your life. _____

_____

_____

_____

_____

_____

_____

For a Christian, _____ is one of those defining moments. When we were baptized, we identified ourselves with _____ and other _____ who had gone before us. We remember who performed the baptism, the faces in the crowd, the temperature of the water, and the location. We made a public declaration of what had taken place in our lives. It was a rich day full of significant meaning.

When we have the opportunity to lead someone to Christ, we also have the privilege to help him or her experience the life-defining act of _____ and begin the process of Christian _____. Usually, a FAITH team makes that follow-up visit the week after the person has accepted Christ. You will want to visit that person to discuss making his or her decision public and following Christ in baptism. If you used A *Step of Faith* leaflet, you have already encouraged the individual to make a public declaration and have introduced the idea of baptism.

ENCOURAGING BAPTISM

Some new believers will not hesitate at the suggestion of baptism. However, for others you will need to spend time explaining the importance of baptism. You and your team need to be sensitive to the Holy Spirit, seeking to discern how to best address this subject. You don't want to take this step lightly or give an inadequate explanation of what baptism means and represents.

A person may be _____ to be baptized for a number of reasons. Crowds, an unbelieving family, and no church background can all contribute to a person's apprehension. We have to take people where they are and help them move _____ in their spiritual journey. Helping them follow through with baptism is a simple way we can help them move forward.

You may need to involve parents and other family members in the discussion of baptism. When dealing with children, respect the wishes of the parents. Baptism is a step of _____ and not a requirement for salvation.

MAKING THE FOLLOW-UP VISIT

If you are returning to visit a person who has not yet been baptized, begin by reacquainting yourself and celebrating the person's _____ to accept Christ. Remind the person of the significance of his or her decision to trust Christ.

Call attention to "Next Steps" on panel 5 of A *Step of Faith* if the new believer has that leaflet available. Ask whether the person has had an opportunity to read that information. Highlight the word *baptism* on that panel. State that baptism is an important _____ _____ in being obedient to Christ after salvation.

Share a brief _____ about the significance of baptism. Sharing your testimony will help someone connect with you, ease fears, and provide a point of reference for future discussion.

In day 5 of last week's "My FAITH Journey" you were asked to develop a baptism testimony. Look back at page 142 and identify the three sections of this testimony.

1. _____

2 _____

3. _____

INTRODUCING *NEXT STEPS IN FOLLOWING JESUS*

Next, transition into a more detailed discussion about baptism by saying, "I'd like to share with you more information about this important next step in your faith journey." Show the person a copy of *Next Steps in Following Jesus*. Briefly call attention to the title. Explain that you will use this leaflet to help the person better understand some next steps of _____ to take as a believer.

BAPTISM is the way we publicly announce what Jesus has done in our lives.

JESUS WAS BAPTIZED OUT OF OBEDIENCE TO HIS FATHER.

"After Jesus was baptized, He went up immediately from the water. The heavens suddenly opened for Him, and He saw the Spirit of God descending like a dove and coming down on Him. And there came a voice from heaven: 'This is My beloved Son. I take delight in Him!'"

Matthew 3:16-17

BAPTISM DEMONSTRATES *YOUR* OBEDIENCE AS WELL.

WHO IS TO BE BAPTIZED?

You are to be baptized if—

• you have trusted Jesus as your Savior;

• you know that baptism is a symbol of what Jesus has done for you and is an expression of obedience to Christ;

• you are not ashamed to follow Christ's example.

2

Open *Next Steps* to panel 2. Call attention to the statement that _____ is one way a Christian publicly shares what Jesus has done for us. Using the leaflet, highlight the significance of believer's baptism as an act of obedience. Emphasize that baptism is for individuals who—

• have already trusted Jesus as _____;
• understand that baptism does not bring salvation but is a _____ of what Jesus has already done for them and is an expression of obedience;
• are not ashamed to follow Christ's _____.

Point out panel 3, "Why Be Baptized?" Although you do not need to read the information from the leaflet, be familiar enough with the content to overview it clearly, referring to the leaflet for supporting Scriptures:

- _____ commanded it.
- Baptism is an act of _____ for which Jesus Himself, as well as His followers, set the example.
- Baptism pictures breaking from the past and beginning a _____ _____ with Christ.
- In the New Testament, baptism is a public _____ of faith.

As time allows, you may want to help the person realize that baptism is a picture of what Jesus has done for a believer. By pointing out some of the elements of baptism, you clarify its beauty, symbolism, and significance.

Call attention to the fact that baptism is by _____ in water. Because it is a public expression of faith, baptism is conducted in front of _____, not a private ceremony. Both Christians, who share baptism as a common experience, and nonbelievers, who have yet to turn from sin to Christ, are encouraged to watch as the person gives a testimony of his new relationship with Jesus.

> ## WHY BE BAPTIZED?
> Every follower of Jesus should be baptized because …
>
> **1. JESUS COMMANDED IT.**
> "Go, therefore, and make disciples of all nations, baptizing them." Matthew 28:19
>
> **2. BAPTISM DEMONSTRATES OBEDIENCE.**
> - Jesus set the example. Mark 1:9
> - Jesus' followers obeyed His command to be baptized. Acts 2:41; 8:38
>
> **3. BAPTISM REPRESENTS A PICTURE OF BREAKING FROM THE PAST AND BEGINNING A NEW LIFE WITH CHRIST.**
> "We were buried with Him by baptism into death, in order that, just as Christ was raised from the dead by the glory of the Father, so we too may walk in a new way of life." Romans 6:4
>
> **4. IN THE NEW TESTAMENT, BAPTISM IS A PUBLIC TESTIMONY OF FAITH.**
> "Those who accepted his message [about Jesus] were baptized." Acts 2:41
>
> **3**

Emphasize the importance of being baptized as _____ as _____. Highlight the importance of being baptized only after _____ accepting Jesus as Savior. Stress the importance of baptism as a point of _____ with other church members.

You may want to ask if the person is willing to take this step of obedience. Use the person's name when asking; for example, "Tony, will you now follow Jesus by being baptized?"

Answer the person's _____ about the reasons for and logistics of baptism. Explain how baptism is done in your church, including where to meet, what to bring, and who baptizes people in your church.

Some churches and FAITH teams show _____ by accompanying the new believer into the baptismal pool. If this is the practice in your church, explain how this works and ask, "Would you allow us the honor and privilege of accompanying you in this wonderful next step of faith—baptism?"

Find out whether the person has a preferred _____ for the baptismal service. Record that information in "About Your Baptism" on panel 5. Explain that the request will be shared, followed up on, and confirmed in a few days by a minister of the church. Share your pastor's name; even though he may not be the minister who performs the baptismal service, the new believer needs to know his name.

Be sure to record all of the requested information in "Appointment for Baptism" on panels 6 and 7, which you tear off and return to the _____. Encourage the individual to think about _____ someone, perhaps an unsaved friend, to his baptismal service.

ABOUT YOUR BAPTISM

Preferred date _____

Place you will meet others

_____

Time to meet _____

5

APPOINTMENT FOR BAPTISM

Name _____

Preferred date _____

Contact number _____

E-mail _____

PRAYER REQUESTS

_____

_____

_____

_____

_____

6

PEOPLE WHO MADE THE VISIT

_____

_____

_____

NOTES

_____

_____

_____

_____

_____

_____

_____

_____

_____

_____

_____

_____

_____

_____

7

NEXT STEPS

God wants you to grow in your relationship with Him. Following Jesus in believer's baptism is one important next step. Here are some other important next steps that will help you become more like Jesus.

PRAYER

In prayer you talk with and listen to Holy God. Prayer should become a way of life, as natural as breathing.

BIBLE STUDY

God teaches us through prayer and through His Word, the Bible. In Bible study, on your own and with others in a Bible-study class, you will learn how to follow Him day by day.

DEVOTIONAL LIFE

Setting aside time every day for prayer and personal Bible study will make a difference in your Christian life. Many people keep a journal so that they can look back and see the ways God answers their prayers.

4

CHURCH WITH BELIEVERS

In most cases people become members of the church in which they are baptized. Fellowship with other Christians in a church will help you grow in your faith. You will make new friends, learn to worship and serve God, and discover more about God's plan for your life. God uses His church to accomplish His purposes throughout the world.

SHARING JESUS WITH OTHERS

The salvation God has given you is too valuable to keep to yourself. Telling others what Jesus has done for you is very powerful.

ABOUT YOUR BAPTISM

Preferred date _____

Place you will meet others

_____

Time to meet _____

5

Explain that baptism is one of several steps in following Jesus. Briefly highlight panels 4 and 5 in the *Next Steps* leaflet to show how these disciplines can help the new believer _____ in Christ. Mention opportunities that are available in your church for him as well as for the entire family, if appropriate. Give the leaflet to the person and conclude the visit with _____.

Return panels 6 and 7, "Appointment for Baptism," to the person in your church who handles FAITH _____ information. Be sure to record, on the Visit Assignment Card or other assignment form, appropriate information that needs to be shared with the church staff about the person's decision.

GROWTH IS A PROCESS

Some new Christians may fail to _____ _____ after making a commitment to come to your Sunday School or worship service. Remember, they may be new to matters of faith, so don't be discouraged. Here are some reasons this may happen.

- They may forget.
- Their family may ask them to attend their church instead of yours.
- The person's spouse may be hostile to their decision to accept Christ and attend church.
- An emergency may arise, such as illness or a change in work schedule.
- Some may fear the unknown.
- In rare cases the profession was insincere. The person may have prayed to receive Christ in order to please you or to get rid of you. If this happens, carefully evaluate how well you are establishing rapport with lost persons before making the FAITH presentation.

Your team is still responsible for helping this person grow as a _____. If this happens, try to _____ _____ to learn what happened, to offer ministry or counsel, and to make sure the new believer gets off to a good start in his new life in Christ. Share information you discover with appropriate staff members.

MY FAITH CONNECTIONS

Visitation Summary

Attempts _____
Completed visits _____
Key Question asked _____

Record a synopsis of your team's visits. Include actions you may need to take on needs discovered. Whom should you tell about these needs? Prayer partners? Sunday School teacher? Minister?

_____

_____

_____

_____

Life-Witness Summary

Key Question asked _____

_____

_____

_____

_____

My Journey This Week

What has God taught you this week? Record insights you have gained about God and yourself.

_____

_____

_____

_____

To-Do List

- ☐ Read session 10
- ☐ Completed "My FAITH Journey":
  - ☐ Day 1
  - ☐ Day 2
  - ☐ Day 3
  - ☐ Day 4
  - ☐ Day 5

- ☐ **Began to pray about my role in FAITH next semester**
- ☐ **Contacted prayer partners**
- ☐ **Practiced FAITH presentation with a friend**
- ☐ _____
- ☐ _____
- ☐ _____
- ☐ _____
- ☐ _____
- ☐ _____

Prayer List

Lost people for whom you are praying:
- ☐ _____
- ☐ _____
- ☐ _____
- ☐ _____
- ☐ _____
- ☐ _____
- ☐ _____
- ☐ _____
- ☐ _____
- ☐ _____
- ☐ _____

Others needing prayer:
- ☐ _____
- ☐ _____
- ☐ _____
- ☐ _____
- ☐ _____
- ☐ _____
- ☐ _____
- ☐ _____
- ☐ _____
- ☐ _____
- ☐ _____

DAY 1

My Faith Journey

A Testimony from Allison

When I was considering making a decision for Jesus, I received a great deal of attention. My Sunday School teacher, my pastor, and a deacon visited and talked with me about it. When I finally made the decision to accept Christ, I shared it with everyone who had visited me. All of a sudden, the contacts stopped. I rarely saw the people who had visited me, except for my Sunday School teacher on Sundays. I became a spiritual orphan, left to figure out the hard stuff on my own.

What emotions is Allison expressing? _____

_____

_____

What expectations are being unmet? _____

_____

_____

_____

Would you consider Allison the exception or the norm? Why? _____

_____

_____

How did you learn to study your Bible, pray, and spend daily time with God?

_____

_____

_____

Review the introductory paragraphs of session 10. Whenever possible, the person who leads an individual to Christ should also help the person learn the basics of the Christian life. Being a disciple maker involves showing by example, not just sharing information. Many new believers are given study guides or books to help them in their spiritual journeys, but there is no substitute for one-to-one mentoring. Your FAITH team is built on the idea that an experienced person helps two others gain experience in witnessing and visitation. That is the same model we must use to guide new believers.

As you go through the day, think about the things you could teach a new believer. Ask God to help you be an example to new believers and to give you opportunities to encourage and strengthen them.

DAY 2

Ronnie was a college student. He did not grow up going to church but got involved in a weekly Bible study group that met at a fast-food restaurant near the campus. One night on their way back to the dorms, one of the guys attending the Bible study asked Ronnie a simple question: "In your personal opinion, what do you understand it takes for a person to get to heaven and have eternal life?" They talked all night, and just before daybreak Ronnie committed his life to Christ. He went to his friend's church the next Sunday and declared his decision to the church.

Ronnie asked if he could schedule his baptism on homecoming weekend because he played football and knew that would be a great weekend for his baptism. He also asked if he could reserve a room at the church for a reception after the worship service. He sent invitations to each football player and coach. He also invited friends, members of his Bible study group, and his family and friends back home. When homecoming weekend came, almost everyone who got an invitation came to see Ronnie baptized.

At the reception that followed, Ronnie introduced the friend who had asked him the Key Question. Ronnie gave a summary of their discussion and then invited his friend to share what he had told Ronnie. The friend began, saying, "There is a word that can help you understand how the Bible answers that question. That word is *FAITH*. The letter *F* stands for …" The pastor who had baptized Ronnie then offered to visit with anyone who wanted to make that same commitment or know more about Jesus. The next week the restaurant was filled with football players and others who wanted to find out more about what Ronnie had discovered.

Ronnie used his baptism to share with his friends and family about Jesus. Baptism is a great way to introduce others to the truth of the gospel. Some people who would never attend a church service would watch a friend be baptized. Ronnie found a way to use his influence to make a difference in the lives of others.

As you go through the day, think of ways you can encourage new believers to use their baptisms as witnessing opportunities for their friends and relatives.

DAY 3

The leaders of the early church were a diverse group. Matthew was a tax collector. Peter was a Jewish fisher with little formal education. Paul was a well-educated Roman citizen with a Jewish heritage and position. Priscilla and Aquilla were tentmakers. Others who accepted Christ include a Roman military officer, a Samaritan woman with a checkered history, a man born blind, and an Ethiopian government official.

All of these persons were characterized by two things: they accepted Jesus as their Savior, and they declared their commitment through baptism. Although not everyone who professed belief in Jesus was baptized (for example, the thief crucified on the cross next to Jesus), the normal practice was for a believer in Jesus to declare a commitment to Jesus through baptism. When people are baptized after conversion, they identify themselves with all the believers who have gone before them and all who will come after them.

When a couple gets married, they usually exchange rings. The rings are not required for marriage, but they serve as a universal testimony of the couple's commitment to each other. When they exchange wedding rings, they identify with all those who were married before them and all those who will marry after them. Just as a wedding ring serves as the recognizable standard that each spouse is part of a family, baptism also serves as the recognizable symbol that a person is part of God's family. Neither a ring nor baptism is required, but both are recognized as significant symbols with rich meaning.

Consider what your baptism meant to those before you and to those who will come after you. Thank God for giving us a simple but meaningful act that declares our trust in Him.

DAY 4

James had been a Christian for a long time. One Sunday he shocked everyone. As the pastor offered an opportunity to respond during the service, James came forward and took the pastor's hand. Everyone assumed he had come forward with a prayer request, but then he sat down on the front row and talked with one of the other ministers. After the response time ended, the pastor introduced James and handed him a microphone. James told of his conversion about 50 years earlier. He also shared about his fear of crowds, especially when he was younger. Because of this fear, he had been reluctant to be baptized. He kept putting it off until he was too embarrassed to follow through with it. James had served on various church committees, had been a Sunday School teacher, and had been involved in numerous church ministries. All those years he had hidden his fear and embarrassment about baptism.

James went on to explain that his failure to be baptized had affected other areas of his spiritual life. For example, his disobedience had affected his relationships with new believers. He had even avoided them, knowing they might ask questions about baptism. In some cases he had resented some new believers who seemed eager to be baptized. James's fear had also impeded his desire to witness. He had rarely shared a verbal witness for Christ, fearing that someone might ask him about baptism, and he would not have been able to tell them about something he had never done.

James's failure to follow Jesus in this simple way had become a big roadblock in his spiritual life. He asked the church to support him as he finally sought to win this battle and be baptized.

If you have not followed through with baptism, pray about taking that next step. If you have already been baptized, how could James's story help a new believer understand the importance of baptism?

_____

_____

_____

_____

_____

_____

_____

_____

DAY 5

MY FAITH JOURNEY

What do you want to happen in your church in the next five years?

_____

_____

_____

What do you want to happen in your family in the next five years?

_____

_____

_____

What do you want to happen in your community in the next five years?

_____

_____

These questions allow you to dream and chart what might happen. Obviously, some of the things you have written are beyond your control.

Draw a wavy line under the things that are beyond your control. The ones that remain are the things you have control over. Here's the hard question: what role are you willing to take to make sure the things within your control come to pass in the next five years?

_____

_____

_____

You have important roles to play in your church, your family, and your community. With God's strength you can make a difference in all three areas. The lives of Abraham, Moses, and Peter remind us that God can use ordinary people to make a major difference in our world. All three of these men had a role to play in God's plans, and so do you and I. God invites each of us to make a difference. The contribution each of us makes is important and full of meaning. In session 11 we will examine the role you can play in helping your church be more effective in leading people to Christ and in building His kingdom.

Consider the difference you are making in the lives of people with whom you come in contact. Thank God for inviting you to play a part in His redemptive purpose in the world.

SESSION

YOUR ROLE IN KINGDOM WORK

SESSION GOALS

You will—
- understand what today's unchurched people seek;
- identify characteristics of a healthy church;
- reflect on ways God uses you in His work;
- better understand the nature of Sunday School and the way your class engages people.

Every church has many unsung heroes. They make sure the grass is mowed and the bus is travel-worthy. Others make sure guests are greeted and can find their way through the church facilities.

The early church also had a number of unsung _____ who quietly made a contribution to the kingdom of God. One such couple was Aquilla and Priscilla. Having fled Rome most likely to escape persecution, they settled in the city of Corinth, a trade center at that time. When the Apostle Paul arrived in the city, they welcomed him into their home. Because all three were tentmakers, they began to work together. This was more than a business; it served as a way to share Jesus with other people. The business was more than a job; it was tool God used to make an impact on the city of Corinth (see Acts 18:1-4).

In time opposition grew in Corinth, and the threesome moved to Ephesus, another trade center, where they established another tentmaking business (see Acts 18:18-20). Paul did not stay long, but Aquila and Priscilla made Ephesus their new home. As they began to share Jesus with others, they encountered a man named Apollos. Well versed in the Old Testament, Apollos knew Jesus' teachings. However, he didn't understand everything, especially about baptism.

Aquila and Priscilla heard Apollos and invited him into their home, where the couple helped him gain a better understanding of baptism. Apollos would move on to share with others, eventually settling in Corinth with the assistance of his two friends in Ephesus. Apollos would prove to make a difference in the town of Corinth. Through Apollos, Aquila and Priscilla ultimately made a difference in a town they had fled (see Acts 18:24-28).

Eventually, this couple would host a church in their home, which became a center for showing Jesus' _____ to others. No matter where this couple lived, they made a _____ in the lives of others. They always found a way to represent God well in this world (see 1 Cor. 16:19).

This couple had been through a lot together. Through all their travel and experiences, they remained _____ to do the work of God's kingdom. Even when a church didn't exist of which they could be a part, they established one. They always found a way to be involved in a _____. Although it was risky at times, this husband-and-wife team were true heroes because they focused their lives on _____ _____. This focus was revealed by the assistance they provided Paul and Apollos and by their efforts to reach others with the _____.

Aquilla and Priscilla understood what _____ were looking for, and they knew how to build a growing _____ that met those needs. During this session we will discover these things as well.

WHAT THE UNCHURCHED ARE LOOKING FOR IN A CHURCH

Meet Donna C. She could be described as a recently unchurched person.

Donna C. was happy with her life. She met Brian at college in the late 1980s, and they were married in 1991. She felt more blessed with the birth of two daughters.

"I guess I was really beginning to fit the soccer-mom role," Donna told us, "Kari, our oldest daughter, was very involved in the peewee soccer league and dance lessons. I decided to quit my job and devote full time to the kids. Brian was very supportive." Brian's quick-pace promotions gave the family a significant income. The building of their dream home quickly followed.

Donna and Brian's religious background could be described easily: nonexistent. Indeed, the couple represented a growing segment in the profile of religious affiliation in America; they were a second-generation unchurched family. Their parents did not attend church, nor did they encourage their children in any religious direction. Brian had some religious influence from his grandparents, but it was minimal. ...

Brian ... left Donna to move in with Susan, his coworker. The divorce left Donna and the girls feeling very alone. Almost in desperation she began attending a Bible study her mother had joined. Donna was unaware at this point that her mother had become a Christian.

The tragic story does have some points of joy. Donna became a Christian. Nine months later she met Ted in a single-again Sunday School class, and they recently announced their engagement.[1]

Two major factors prompted Donna to try a church: a _____ in her life and a _____ with someone who was active in the church. Donna was immediately drawn to a _____ _____, even though she had no background in understanding the Bible. Someone from the church she eventually joined shared with Donna how to become a Christian. The pastor and his preaching were also key factors in Donna's acceptance of Christ and her choice of this church. The Bible study class Donna joined helped her assimilate into the church quickly and to grow as a Christian.

Donna could be described as a typical unchurched person in America. What issues do you see that may be concerns for all unchurched people?

_____

_____

What do you think the unchurched are looking for in a church? _____

_____

_____

_____

People in general, especially young adults, want a place where they can—
- discover the _____;
- find _____;
- enjoy a variety of _____;
- have an opportunity to make a _____ in the world.

If we are going to reach today's young adults and others who need the Lord (and may not even know it yet), we must find ways to make these four things happen.

What can your church do in these four areas to help reach the unchurched?

Discover the truth: _____

_____

_____

_____

Find connections: _____

_____

_____

_____

Enjoy a variety of experiences: _____

_____

_____

_____

Make a difference in the world: _____

_____

_____

_____

BUILDING A HEALTHY CHURCH

Most of these characteristics can be seen in the lives of Aquila and Priscilla. Their commitment to the _____ of Scripture can be seen in their ability to test the teachings of Apollos. Their relationship with Paul points to a sense of _____. When they first met Apollos, they were in a religious service—a community happening. Scripture never names them separately, a fact that highlights their _____.

Together this couple was involved in the work of _____, opening a tent store as a means to be involved in meeting and interacting with the community. The couple were _____ to Apollos, encouraging him in his spiritual journey. They hosted a _____ in their house as a means to reach their city for Christ. The Bible is silent about the nature of the _____ in their house church, but we can imagine that Paul's involvement in their church didn't hurt their worship! Aquila and Priscilla did their part to ensure that their church was healthy.

Consider the things your church does to ensure health. Identify ways your Sunday School or small group does or could make each of the following things happen.

A commitment to the truth of Scripture: _____

_____

_____

_____

_____

A sense of community: _____

_____

_____

_____

Unity of purpose: _____

_____

_____

A means for everyone to be involved:_____

_____

_____

_____

A focus on spiritual growth: _____

_____

_____

_____

Meaningful worship: _____

_____

_____

_____

Genuine concern for the lost: _____

_____

_____

_____

Engaging believers in the lives of others: _____

_____

_____

A healthy Sunday School or other open Bible study groups will not ensure a healthy church, but it will move a church toward health and ministry. Why? Sunday School and small groups are places where people _____ with one another and the ministry of the church, _____ the truth of God's Word, and _____ others so that they too can discover God's truth.

Giving focus to these three things—_____, _____, and _____—will make your Sunday School and your church a positive force in your community as believers engage in the lives of others. During your daily "My FAITH Journey" assignments this week, you will look more closely at how your church can do these three things.

STORIES FROM THE FIELD

We have already discovered some ways we can be a part of Kingdom work by looking at the example set by Aquilla and Priscilla. Here are some modern-day Aquillas and Priscillas who are finding new ways of being involved in Kingdom work. As you read, listen expectantly as God's Holy Spirit directs you to the opportunities He has for you.

The Bake Team

Leslie is the captain of a team of women who prepare meals for families in their Sunday School department. Her team and five other teams rotate meal preparation for young adults when there is a death, birth, or hospital stay. This week Leslie's team will prepare a meal for a family that is celebrating the birth of their first child.

At the end of Sunday School, the team makes some preliminary plans for the meal. A first-time guest in the class overhears this conversation. She enjoys cooking and is looking for a way to make a difference in the lives of others. She asks Leslie if she can help with the meal. Leslie shares the menu with her and invites her to their cooking party on Tuesday afternoon.

The young woman, Ann, shows up at Leslie's house with the others, and they prepare the meal to be delivered. Leslie invites her newfound cooking partner to accompany her when she delivers the meal, and she accepts.

Leslie and Ann begin to spend time together, sharing recipes and cooking tips. Six weeks later it is Leslie's team's turn to prepare a meal, and once again Ann comes to the cooking party. She and her husband have now enrolled in the Sunday School class and are building new friendships. While they are cooking, Leslie asks if she can ask Ann a simple question. Ann agrees, and Leslie asks, "In your personal opinion, what do you understand it takes for a person to get to heaven and have eternal life?" After a few more conversations Leslie has the privilege of hearing Ann pray a salvation prayer, accepting God's offer of forgiveness. In time Ann will become the leader of another cooking team, inviting others to help her make a difference through cooking.

A Family Reunion

All kinds of activities are going on during the family reunion. Lisa is playing a board game at one table, while her husband sits at another table playing a different board game. As her husband is playing, he overhears Lisa asking the Key Question to one of her cousins as they continue to play their game. Her husband continues to play at his table, but he can't help listening to what is going on at the adjacent table. He hears Lisa ask, "Do you mind if I share with you what I discovered in the Bible?" Aware of what is about to happen, her husband begins to silently pray for his wife as she begins the FAITH gospel presentation. Lisa dialogues with her cousin, progressing from F to H, all the while continuing to play their board game. The conversation ends with the cousin thanking Lisa for sharing. The cousin does not make a decision for Christ, but Lisa leaves the door open for future conversation.

As the games end, another relative approaches Lisa to tell her she has been watching Lisa share with the cousin. Impressed, the relative wants to know how Lisa learned to share her faith. They talk about the FAITH training Lisa attends. Lisa encourages her relative to talk with her pastor about offering evangelism training in their church.

A Community-Service Project

The College Sunday School Department is asked to participate in a local community-service project helping people in the area who have sustained flood damage to their homes. One college student invites his fraternity, which has been looking for a community-service project, to participate as well.

Several church members gather with the frat in the church parking lot. The group is organized, and assignments are made. They head to a home and begin working. As the church members and frat members work together, they talk about all kinds of things. They discover that some of the frat members grew up in church but haven't been involved in a local church since they moved away from home to attend college. A few church members initiate spiritual dialogues with a couple of the frat members, and they make plans to take the two college students out for lunch to continue talking.

A church member discovers that one frat member is having difficulty in a class. The church member, who has a degree in that area, offers to tutor the college student. As they finish the project, they make plans to find another house to work on next month. During the next day's worship service as people greet one another, several church members who worked the day before notice some of the frat guys slipping into the worship service.

STORIES FROM YOUR FIELD

These stories remind us that God uses all kinds of _____ and _____ to involve His followers in Kingdom work. No doubt over the past few weeks, God has used you in Kingdom work.

Write your story from the field. _____

_____

_____

_____

_____

_____

_____

_____

_____

_____

_____

_____

_____

_____

_____

_____

_____

_____

_____

_____

_____

_____

_____

_____

_____

_____

_____

_____

First Corinthians 3:1-9 points out the different roles of Paul and Apollos in sharing the message of salvation. Paul noted in verse 6, "I planted, Apollos watered, but God gave the growth." This verse reminds us of a very important fact about multiplication: it comes as a result of _____ _____, but we must also _____ with _____ to bring it about. Writing to the Ephesian Christians, Paul emphasized this partnership when he wrote that God "is able to do above and beyond all that we ask or think—according to the power that works in you" (Eph. 3:20).

Enjoy the opportunity to be involved in Kingdom work, thanking God for the _____ He allows you to play. Continue to pray and rely on His _____ _____ to discern where He might lead you in the future.

1. Thom S. Rainer, _Surprising Insights from the Unchurched and Proven Ways to Reach Them_ (Grand Rapids, MI: Zondervan, 2001), 17–19.

MY FAITH CONNECTIONS

Visitation Summary

Attempts _____
Completed visits _____
Key Question asked _____

Record a synopsis of your team's visits. Include actions you may need to take on needs discovered. Whom should you tell about these needs? Prayer partners? Sunday School teacher? Minister?

_____

_____

_____

_____

_____

Life-Witness Summary

Key Question asked _____

_____

_____

_____

_____

My Journey This Week

What has God taught you this week? Record insights you have gained about God and yourself.

_____

_____

_____

_____

To-Do List

☐ **Read session 11**
☐ **Completed "My FAITH Journey":**
  ☐ **Day 1**
  ☐ **Day 2**
  ☐ **Day 3**
  ☐ **Day 4**
  ☐ **Day 5**

☐ **Invited at least one person to attend Sunday School with me**
☐ **Contacted prayer partners**
☐ **Prayed about my role in future FAITH training opportunities**
☐ **Practiced FAITH presentation with a friend**
☐ _____
☐ _____
☐ _____
☐ _____
☐ _____

Prayer List

Lost people for whom you are praying:
☐ _____
☐ _____
☐ _____
☐ _____
☐ _____
☐ _____
☐ _____
☐ _____
☐ _____
☐ _____

Others needing prayer:
☐ _____
☐ _____
☐ _____
☐ _____
☐ _____
☐ _____
☐ _____
☐ _____
☐ _____
☐ _____

DAY 1

At the end of session 11 we discovered that different roles may be involved in leading someone to accept Christ. Here is a simple illustration of that truth. Walt, a salesman at a local store, has contact with several members of your church on a weekly basis. He is always impressed with the way they do business with him. A few of them have invited him to attend church with them, even offering to pick him up, and he has attended Bible study a few times.

A FAITH team conducts an Opinion Poll at Walt's home. He listens but does not make a decision. However, Walt accepts an invitation to attend a men's fish fry on Friday evening. During the fish fry, a guest speaker gives fishing tips and closes by explaining how he became a Christian. The pastor then offers to stay and talk with anyone who would like to know more about becoming a Christian. Walt sets an appointment with the pastor and, three days later, accepts Christ as his personal Savior and Lord.

Who led Walt to Jesus? _____

They all did.

Suppose one of the *church members* had bad credit with Walt's store and other businesses. Do you think that would have given Walt pause when he began to get invitations to attend your church? Suppose the *person who invited Walt* had failed to bring him. Suppose the *pastor* had not made himself available to talk. Suppose the *speaker* had shared only fishing tips and had failed to share about his salvation. Everyone had a role to play, and each part was important.

Over the past 11 weeks you too have had opportunities to make a difference in many different ways. Review your "My FAITH Connections" checklists from the previous 10 weeks, giving particular attention to the entries about your visits and your spiritual dialogues day by day.

Identify the different ways the Holy Spirit has used and continues to use you to impact someone in these various encounters. List the different ways you have made and are continuing to make a difference.

_____

_____

_____

_____

_____

_____

You could have included all kinds of things—praying, saying a kind word, introducing someone to Jesus. Each thing you did was important. Take time to thank God for using you to make a difference. Look for one way you can continue to make a difference for God today by being obedient.

DAY 2

According to statistics, "people will come to your Bible study group and to church *if invited*. Many will receive Jesus as their Savior *if invited*. Unfortunately, a disturbing number of these people will drop out" of church if connections are not established.

Research indicates that "people exposed to the gospel a number of times before accepting Christ are more likely to remain active" than those who hear the good news only once or twice before their decision. This same research found that "people who establish friendships with several people in their church within a few months of joining are far more likely to remain active."

Where can a person get connected before and after a decision for Christ? The obvious answer is a Bible study class or another small group. The reason? Healthy classes or groups focus on relationships, helping both members and prospects connect with one another in the group.

In addition, a healthy group or class helps newcomers connect to a specific ministry in which they receive care and nurture and can find ways to make a difference. Such avenues help members connect to Christ's work through His church.

What are some ways your Sunday School or small group helps others connect? Here are a few ideas for making connections:

- Warmly greet everyone on arriving.
- Ask everyone to wear a name tag.
- Give guests an opportunity to join the class or group.
- Take the attendance.
- Pair each guest with a member.
- Gather prayer requests.
- Plan fellowships.
- Organize and maintain functioning care groups.
- Contact absentees weekly.
- Quickly and appropriately address discovered needs.[1]

What are ways your class or group builds stronger connections? _____

_____

_____

_____

Sunday School classes and small groups are places people can go to find friendship and opportunities to make a difference. Ask God to help you make your class or group better connectors. List at least one thing you can do to improve your class or group in this area.

_____

_____

1. Adapted from David Francis, *The 3D Sunday School* (Nashville: LifeWay Press, 2006), and G. Dwayne McCrary, LifeWay conference material.

DAY 3

When you think of Sunday School, what comes to mind? _____

_____

You could have listed many things, but ultimately, the purpose of Sunday School is to help people discover and live the truths of God's Word. As people ask questions in a safe environment, they begin to understand who God is, who they are, and why they need the Savior. The power of Sunday School or any other group with a similar purpose is not its friendliness or an individual's dynamic personality. The power of Sunday School is the study of God's Word.

Thom Rainer has conducted extensive research on the beliefs and behaviors of the unchurched. In his book *The Unchurched Next Door* he revealed some surprising insights from the unchurched:

- More than 17 million Americans will accept Christ if presented with the gospel. Another 43 million are close—possibly open and receptive to the gospel.
- Most unchurched persons believe in the existence of both heaven and hell (79 percent and 70 percent, respectively).
- Unchurched persons are nervous but willing to talk about matters of faith.
- Most of the unchurched have a fairly high view of the Bible. One-third believe it is totally true; another 46 percent believe it is generally true.
- Most of the unchurched would rather talk to a layperson than to a minister about religious matters.
- Many of the unchurched wonder why their Christian neighbors and coworkers do not invite them to church.
- Most of the unchurched have a spiritual view of life.[1]

Which of these findings surprises you the most? Why? _____

_____

_____

Which of these insights could change the way your small group or class functions? Why and how?

_____

_____

_____

The bottom line is that people want to know the truth. Sunday School and small groups give all people a vehicle for discovering God's truths in the comfort of a group of fellow explorers. Thank God for your class or small group. Ask Him to help you find more ways to help others discover God's truths.

1. Thom S. Rainer, *The Unchurched Next Door* (Grand Rapids, MI: Zondervan, 2003), 46–55.

MY FAITH JOURNEY

DAY 4

Dr. Rainer's research reveals some other surprising insights:

- Most of the unchurched prefer to attend on Sunday morning if they attend.
- Most of the unchurched feel guilty about not attending church.
- Eighty-two percent of the unchurched are at least somewhat likely to attend church if they are invited.
- Very few of the unchurched have had someone share with them the way to become a Christian.
- Most of the unchurched have a positive view of pastors, ministers, and the church.
- The unchurched would like to develop a real and sincere relationship with a Christian.
- Many of the unchurched are far more concerned about the spiritual well-being of their children than of themselves.[1]

Why do you think most people attend your church? Because of the dynamic worship experience? A great children's ministry? An exciting student ministry? Special events? Direct mail? An overwhelming amount of research indicates that 80 to 90 percent of people surveyed say they first came to the church they currently attend because someone invited them. The previous list can give members a reason to invite someone, but programs and ministries alone seldom magnetically attract people. What usually happens is the satisfied-customer principle.

Satisfied customers are always the best advertisement for a business. Any marketing expert will tell you customers' word-of-mouth communication is the most common way businesses acquire new customers. Similarly, a person whose needs are met by a church is a satisfied "customer." He or she will invite others to attend, believing the other person will have his or her needs met as well.

When we talk about inviting people, we are not talking about handing out flyers or cards. These have their place, but what we are talking about is inviting a person to go *with you*. That means you may need to pick them up or, at the very least, meet them in the church parking lot and stay with them from that point on.

Sunday School has historically been an intentional evangelistic tool of the church. However, it can be evangelistic only when lost people are present. Sunday School works if churches work their Sunday School.[2]

Of the persons you identified in day 4 of session 1's "My FAITH Journey" (p. 27), how many of them have you invited to attend Sunday School or your small group with you? _____

Identify at least two persons you have been praying for and can invite to attend with you on Sunday.

_____

Now invite them.

1. Thom S. Rainer, *The Unchurched Next Door* (Grand Rapids, MI: Zondervan, 2003), 23–30.
2. Ibid., 245.

DAY 5

Ezra was an Old Testament prophet God used to bring revival. Introduced in Scripture as a scribe, Ezra would have had intimate knowledge of the Old Testament law (see Ezra 7:6). He is also described as one who "had determined in his heart to study the law of the Lord, obey it, and teach its statutes and ordinances in Israel" (Ezra 7:10). He was committed to learning the truths of God and to making sure others could learn these truths as well.

The Jewish people had been conquered and led away in exile, and some had now returned to Jerusalem to rebuild the temple. When Ezra arrived in Jerusalem after the temple had been rebuilt, he offered a sacrifice to God and delivered a message from the king. The leaders of the Israelites approached Ezra to tell him they had disobeyed God's commands by marrying non-Jewish women.

The problem with these women wasn't their race as much as the fact that they continued to worship their gods and introduced these pagan practices to the Jews. Ezra was heartbroken when he learned about this problem (see Ezra 9:3) because, in effect, the Israelites were headed toward the same destruction they had just experienced. As he lay on the ground pouring out his heart to God, a crowd gathered around him. Ezra's weeping was interrupted by one of the leaders, who confessed that the people of Israel had sinned. This leader closed his address to Ezra with a challenge, saying, "Get up, for this matter is your responsibility, and we support you. Be strong and take action!" (Ezra 10:4).

God had used Ezra to expose the people's sin, and now it was Ezra's responsibility to lead them to action. Knowledge always leads to responsibility. James wrote, "For the person who knows to do good and doesn't do it, it is a sin" (Jas. 4:17).

You have learned a great deal over the past 11 weeks. Now you have a responsibility to use that knowledge. Using what you have learned includes training others to do the things you have done, including witnessing. In session 12 we will look more closely at your stewardship as a trained witness for Jesus.

Ask God to show you what you are to do with the knowledge you have gained these past 11 weeks. Thank Him for the experiences and new relationships He has brought into your life.

SESSION

YOUR NEXT STEP

SESSION GOALS

You will—
- state the importance of preparing the next generation of FAITH participants;
- affirm that, as a Christ-follower, you are already a leader and can assume a leadership role;
- outline a biblical pattern for training others;
- accept your stewardship of what you have learned and experienced in FAITH training;
- identify lessons you can pass on to others.

Reginald Jones was one of the most influential people in the business world during the 1970s. As the CEO of General Electric (GE), he was the standard by which all other corporate leaders were evaluated. In his second year as CEO, Jones began the process of selecting his successor. He began with a list of 96 candidates, all inside GE. Over a two-year time period he narrowed that group to 12. Then he reduced the group to half. Over the next few years these six individuals were assigned different sectors of the company to manage, and their performance was evaluated. In 1980 Jones retired and handed over the company to Jack Welch, one of the six sector executives. Other companies hired the other five to serve as their CEOs.

Of Jones's eight years as CEO, he spent seven preparing his successor. Knowing he would one day retire, Jones invested time and energy in the future leaders who would carry on the GE legacy after he was gone.

The test of a leader is his ability to pass on his _____ and _____ to those who will come after him. All leaders must face the reality that someday they will no longer be able to do what they have done. Paul reminded his hearers that even the great King David died after serving God's purposes in his generation (see Acts 13:36). It happens to the best of them. The same is true of FAITH training. Now that you are approaching the end of this semester, you must think about ways you can _____ _____ what you have learned to others.

This is not a new idea. Moses served as a mentor to Joshua and passed off the leadership of the Hebrews to him (see Deut. 31). Jesus trained His disciples to carry on His ministry after His death and resurrection; He prayed about this matter with His disciples just hours prior to His crucifixion (see John 17:6-19). Barnabas mentored a young Mark (see Acts 15:36-39). Paul prepared the next generation of ministers, including Timothy and Titus.

You have seen this pattern modeled by the persons who have taught you, as well as by your FAITH team leader. The idea of sharing what is learned is an essential part of the FAITH strategy. But its roots go deeper than that. During this session we will examine every believer's responsibility to pass on what he or she has learned so that the number of growing, witnessing believers is _____.

SHARING WHAT YOU HAVE BEEN GIVEN

We know a lot about Paul. Here is some of what we know.
- He was well educated by Gamaliel (see 5:34; Acts 22:3).
- He grew up in a religious structure (see Acts 26:5).
- He was zealous about his beliefs even when wrong (see Gal. 1:14).
- He had a unique conversion experience (see Acts 9).
- He spent time learning from the apostles (see Acts 9:27).
- He invested his life in future leaders (see 2 Tim. 2:2).

It's important to note that Paul spent time being mentored by the apostles. He then invested that same learning in the lives of others, most notably Timothy.

Timothy had a strong heritage as well; both his mother and his grandmother were known for their faith (see 2 Tim. 1:5). They had passed on that heritage to young Timothy, and Paul built on what they had taught. When Paul wrote 1 and 2 Timothy, he was in prison and knew he was about to die. He wrote the two letters to Timothy to give his young protégé the final instructions he would need to be successful in Kingdom work. In the middle of the second letter, Paul challenged Timothy to pass the torch to others, stating, "What you have heard from me in the presence of many witnesses, commit to faithful men who will be able to teach others also" (2 Tim. 2:2).

The FAITH strategy follows the pattern Paul presented to Timothy. We can use
_____ ____ to help us better understand what is involved in passing on the
things we have learned and experienced.

1._____ (learn): "what you have heard from me."
Perhaps you can recall being in school when someone asked, "Do we have to know
this?" Basically, the person wanted to know whether the subject would be on a test,
as if it would be memorized for the test and then quickly forgotten.

Unlike this type of "learning," growing as a FAITH practitioner requires that you
continually receive. You are always in a position to learn, especially from God's
_____. And it's not enough just to listen; you must put into practice what
you've learned (see Luke 6:46-49; Jas. 1:22). You can never be _____ in
your Christian walk, thinking you have arrived. God wants you to experience Him
_____. You must learn more about yourself and more about Him every day.

In addition to learning from God's Word each day, you should learn from other
Bible-based material as well. J. Oswald Sanders writes, "Leaders should determine
to spend a minimum of half an hour a day reading books that feed the soul and
stimulate the mind."[1] Participating in additional FAITH training, reading, and
attending conferences can also help you grow as a follower of Jesus.

2._____ (teach): "commit to faithful men."
In *Share Jesus Without Fear* William Fay explains why so many Christians do not
share their faith with others. He says that even many long-time believers often
claim, "I don't know enough." Fay insists that these believers know plenty, but they
keep taking in spiritual truth without sharing that truth.

Although you may have been participating this semester as a learner, in reality
you are already a spiritual _____ whom God has entrusted with much. As
you have been reminded during FAITH training, you recognize that the salvation
you have received from God is not to be kept to yourself but shared with those who
need it. In the same way, you must _____ what you have learned with others
who can use their training to reach the lost for Christ.

3._____ (train): "who will be able to teach others also."
Throughout history, master craftsmen have taken on apprentices who worked
with them for little or nothing, not only doing menial tasks but also learning the
trade and how to teach it to others. After a number of years in training, these
apprentices went out on their own to earn a living and train their own apprentices.
For centuries this process was repeated, but with a few exceptions it is rarely
followed in occupations today.

The same can be said of spiritual training. Although some believers still learn
truth and share it with others, many don't guide other believers to train those who
come after them. For example, in many large Sunday School classes a gifted teacher
focuses more on telling than on reproducing those who can train others. Sharing
the truth of the Word is important, but it is also important to _____
others to share the truth and to teach others to do the same. This is what making
_____ is all about. One implication of Jesus' Great Commission is that
to make disciples, Jesus' followers must _____ our lives through the
lives of others. In fact, multiplying believers is the way the church grows. Without
multiplication the church would cease to exist.

STEWARDS OF A GIFT

Paul challenged Timothy to fulfill his ministry. In doing so, he reminded Timothy of the _____ of his call (see 2 Tim. 4:5). Paul had been a faithful steward of what had been passed on to him. He understood that mentors receive their pay by seeing their pupils _____ and continue the cycle, mentoring others. Paul had the responsibility to pass on to others what had been given to him, and he challenged Timothy to do the same.

Many times it appears that we don't think about what has been given to us by those who invested their lives in us, teaching us how to live the Christian life. They didn't have to show us the things they did, but they realized they were stewards of what had been given to them.

When we receive a gift, certain _____ are associated with that gift:
1. We have been entrusted with a _____ gift.
2. We are given gifts for a _____ or a reason.
3. Purposeful gifts imply a _____.
4. Stewardship always carries _____.
5. Accountability and stewardship affect areas _____ to the gift.

Imagine that someone gives you a watch. A watch is a great gift—something you can use every day. Time is valuable, and having a watch can help you redeem that commodity. Most likely, the person who gave you the watch gave it to you on purpose. Either your old watch is broken or worn out, or you may just need a reminder to be on time.

Your receiving the watch implies that you will use it (a stewardship). The person didn't give it to you expecting it to remain wrapped or never to be worn. They expect you to use the watch. Eventually, they will notice whether you are wearing the watch. If you are not wearing it, you will probably be asked why. If you fail to use the watch, you are in danger of hurting a friend and damaging a relationship.

These same principles can be applied to the gift God has given us in His Son. Is He a great gift?   ☐ Yes   ☐ No

Explain your answer. _____

_____

_____

_____

What was the reason behind the gift? _____

_____

_____

What is the stewardship involved with receiving the Son? _____

_____

_____

In what ways does God hold us accountable for using the gift? _____

_____

_____

_____

How does the gift of the Son affect all areas of our lives? _____

_____

_____

_____

WHAT CAN I OFFER?

God has entrusted us with many great _____. Certain _____ are associated with each one. Paul and Timothy had much to offer the next generation. For example, Paul was well educated and had some specialized training. He had a wide range of experiences, to say the least. Timothy had a strong family heritage. He had been given a relationship with Paul and also had some unique experiences. Obviously, these men had something to pass on to the next generation.

What about you and me? What do we have to pass on to the next _____ of FAITH participants? Let's think about that for a moment.

How would you describe your family heritage? _____

_____

_____

What training and wisdom have you received? _____

_____

_____

Whom has God used to mold and shape you in your spiritual walk? _____

_____

_____

What experiences has God used to teach you more about Him? _____

_____

_____

_____

You have something to pass on to the next generation of _____ _____.
If you fail to pass it on, the next generation will never be able to accomplish what it could have for the kingdom of God. God has given each of us unique experiences and opportunities that _____ _____ can share. What qualified Paul and Timothy to pass on what they had learned also qualifies you and me—God's invitation to be part of His kingdom work.

Your responses to the following may help you discover the kingdom work God wants you to do.

Name five significant events in your walk with God.

1. _____

2. _____

3. _____

4. _____

5. _____

In what ways has God recently worked in your life, especially through your involvement in FAITH?

_____

_____

_____

_____

_____

_____

_____

What would you like your church to do to reach the lost and multiply disciples?

_____

_____

_____

_____

_____

_____

Considering your gifts and experiences, what role could you play in making that happen?

_____

_____

_____

_____

_____

_____

_____

As you evaluate your response to these questions, look for common elements. God has given you these experiences and desires for a reason. Think about ways you can make a difference in the lives of others.

How do you think God can use you to make a difference in others' lives through your future involvement in FAITH? Check one or more options or write your own.
❏ *Become a FAITH team leader*
❏ *Participate in another semester of FAITH training*
❏ *Other:* _____

_____

_____

What specific steps will you take to pass on to others what God has taught you through this semester of FAITH?

_____

_____

_____

_____

_____

_____

_____

_____

_____

God has allowed you to learn some valuable lessons during the past 12 weeks. Compare them to the discoveries Harvey Penick made in his life.

Harvey Penick was the head golf professional at Austin Country Club from 1923 until 1973 and the golf coach at the University of Texas from 1931 to 1963. In 1989 the PGA of America honored Penick as teacher of the year. He was known for carrying a red notebook in which he recorded golf tips, insights, and stories. Several different people had tried to persuade him to publish the contents of his red notebook, but he had refused. No one except his son had ever read the notebook, and Penick's plan was to pass the notebook on to his son after he died. However, one day Penick began to wonder whether it was wrong for him to keep everything he had learned to himself. As he reflected on his 87 years of life, he wondered whether he had been granted all those experiences to pass on to others. Penick concluded that he had not been given his experiences and expertise to be kept a secret. Penick contacted a writer to help him organize the notebook, which was published as *The Little Red Book*. It became the most popular golf book ever published.

During these weeks of FAITH training, you have seen evidence of God's grace and power. You have learned more about being a disciple and a witness. Your faith in God has been stretched and strengthened. You have a choice: you can enjoy these insights and your deeper faith, keeping them all for yourself, or you can ask yourself the same questions considered by Harvey Penick. Has God allowed you to learn and experience these things for a _____? Does He want you to _____ _____ to the next generation of FAITH learners the things you have learned?

Many people have yet to be told about _____. Others are waiting to learn how to share Jesus with a _____. You can help them. The question is not whether you _____ help but whether you _____ help. May God motivate and empower us pass on what we have received as we seek to make disciples in a world that desperately needs the Savior.

1. J. Oswald Sanders, with contributions by Neil Knierim and Yvonne Burrage, *Spiritual Leadership: Responding to God's Call* (Nashville: LifeWay Press, 1999), 90.

MY FAITH CONNECTIONS

Visitation Summary

Attempts _____
Completed visits _____
Key Question asked _____

Record a synopsis of your team's visits. Include actions you may need to take on needs discovered. Whom should you tell about these needs? Prayer partners? Sunday School teacher? Minister?

_____

_____

_____

_____

_____

Life-Witness Summary

Key Question asked _____

_____

_____

_____

_____

My Journey This Week

What has God taught you this week? Record insights you have gained about God and yourself.

_____

_____

_____

_____

To-Do List

- ☐ Read session 12
- ☐ Completed "My FAITH Journey":
  - ☐ Day 1
  - ☐ Day 2
  - ☐ Day 3
  - ☐ Day 4
  - ☐ Day 5

- ☐ Prayed about my role in future FAITH training opportunities
- ☐ Contacted prayer partners
- ☐ Practiced FAITH presentation
- ☐ Contacted church leader about availability to share FAITH experiences with others
- ☐ Encouraged others to enroll in FAITH training
- ☐ _____
- ☐ _____
- ☐ _____
- ☐ _____

Prayer List

Lost people for whom you are praying:
- ☐ _____
- ☐ _____
- ☐ _____
- ☐ _____
- ☐ _____
- ☐ _____
- ☐ _____
- ☐ _____
- ☐ _____
- ☐ _____
- ☐ _____

Others needing prayer:
- ☐ _____
- ☐ _____
- ☐ _____
- ☐ _____
- ☐ _____
- ☐ _____
- ☐ _____
- ☐ _____
- ☐ _____

DAY 1

God has no doubt taught you many things over the past 12 weeks. Review the "My Journey This Week" section of each week's "My FAITH Connections" checklist. Write insights you gained in the following areas.

Things I learned about myself: _____

_____

_____

_____

_____

_____

_____

Things I learned about God: _____

_____

_____

_____

_____

_____

_____

Things I learned about the lost: _____

_____

_____

_____

_____

_____

_____

Review what you wrote and consider who else needs to know these things. How would they benefit from knowing these things? How could you pass on the insights you have gained?

MY FAITH JOURNEY

DAY 2

Paul wrote to the Philippians, "Not that I have already reached the goal or am already fully mature, but I make every effort to take hold of it because I also have been taken hold of by Christ Jesus. Brothers, I do not consider myself to have taken hold of it. But one thing I do: forgetting what is behind and reaching forward to what is ahead, I pursue as my goal the prize promised by God's heavenly call in Christ Jesus. Therefore, all who are mature should think this way. And if you think differently about anything, God will reveal this to you. In any case, we should live up to whatever truth we have attained" (Phil. 3:12-16).

God used Paul's pen to write half of the New Testament. The hardships Paul endured testify to his commitment to spread the gospel of Christ. His impact on the early church is unquestionable. If anyone ran the good race that is the Christian life, it was Paul. Yet in this passage Paul declared that he still had more to learn.

If Paul could not say he had arrived, neither can we. An exciting reality about Christianity is that there is always more to learn and apply to our lives. The standard is not ourselves or other Christians but the One we follow—Jesus. He is the standard, and until we meet His standard, we still have more work to do.

You have learned a great deal over the past 12 weeks, but God still has more for you to learn and become. But spiritual growth does not happen by accident. You must continue putting yourself in a position to grow in your relationship with God. Prayer, obedience to and dependence on the Holy Spirit, fasting, Bible study, worship, service, witnessing, and journaling are a few ways you can put yourself in a position to encounter God and allow Him to transform you in Christlikeness.

What can you do to put yourself in a position to encounter God? _____

_____

_____

_____

_____

_____

_____

_____

Who can hold you accountable for doing these things? _____

_____

Think about reading a book on spiritual disciplines, such as *Celebration of Discipline: The Path to Spiritual Growth* by Richard Foster, *The Disciplines of the Spirit* by Dallas Willard, or *Spiritual Disciplines for the Christian Life* by Donald S. Whitney. LifeWay Christian Resources offers the Growing Disciples Series, which teaches six essential disciplines of the Christian life. The seven books in the series can be studied by individuals or groups.

DAY 3

Read the following scenarios and write a way you, as a trained FAITH witness, could help in each situation.

As your Sunday School teacher teaches a lesson about death, several attendees ask questions about salvation. They also ask whether they can meet with the teacher in the next few days to talk more about what it means to be a Christian.

_____

_____

During the response time during the worship service, several persons come forward to talk to the pastor. He tries to quickly minister to the needs of each person while the others patiently wait.

_____

_____

A friend has a son who is asking questions about spiritual things. The mom is doing her best to answer the questions but is having trouble helping him find answers in the Bible.

_____

_____

During the annual Christmas pageant attendees are asked to complete a survey about the pageant. One question asks about church involvement. The surveys reveal that many people do not have church homes. Because the Christmas season is so busy, weekly visitation is on hold, so the church staff is trying to contact before Christmas every person without a church home.

_____

_____

Even though this semester of FAITH training is over, the need to share Jesus is never over. You have many opportunities to continue making a difference. Contact your pastor, Sunday School leaders, or other church leaders and offer to help as needed. Ask God to help you find ways to continue sharing the good news with the lost and to continue making disciples.

List three ways you can continue to be involved in witnessing and disciple making.

1. _____
2. _____
3. _____

MY FAITH JOURNEY

DAY 4

Another FAITH semester will begin soon, bringing new things to learn, new people to meet, new experiences, and new opportunities to sharpen your skills as a witness. A new semester also presents the opportunity to pass on the things you have learned. You can be involved in FAITH training in a variety of ways. Pray especially about one of these areas:

1. *FAITH team leader.* Leading a team is the ideal next step for someone who has completed *FAITH Evangelism* 1. You would lead a team of three (including yourself), passing on what you have learned to the other members of your team. *FAITH Evangelism* 2 provides essential training for FAITH team leaders.

2. *FAITH team learner.* In addition to new learners, some choose to continue in FAITH as learners for more than one semester, taking on additional responsibilities and assisting the team leader.

For the FAITH process to work, team leaders are essential. The more team leaders available, the greater number of people who can be involved in FAITH training. The FAITH process depends on learners becoming leaders. Maybe the thought of being a leader makes you nervous, as you might have been during your first week of FAITH training. But just as God helped you as a learner, He can help you as a leader.

Although leading a team is the ideal next step, you can pass on what you have learned and received in other ways, such as prayer, Sunday School leadership, and training. Be responsive to the opportunities offered by your church and to God's leadership in your life. Recognize your role as a leader in your church and in FAITH, with the opportunity to pass on what you have learned and to mentor others. Training will be available to help you continue growing as a disciple.

Pray about the role you will play in the next semester of FAITH. Contact your FAITH administrator, your pastor, or your minister of education and let him know of your desire to be involved.

DAY 5

In session 1 we learned about the need for change in our world. We discovered that every hour in the United States, an average of 214 people die without Christ.[1] In session 4 we discovered that the greatest need in this world can be summed up in one way: forgiveness through Christ only.

You saw spiritual needs as you made visits and developed relationships with lost people. Jesus' words about the abundant harvest are more alive to you today than ever: "The harvest is abundant," Jesus said in Matthew 9:37. We hope you have discovered that many are ready to accept the truth of the gospel if they are told and are given the opportunity to do so.

In the same passage Jesus also said that "the workers are few. Therefore, pray to the Lord of the harvest to send out workers into His harvest" (Matt. 9:37-38). Aware of the need, He called for His followers to pray for more workers. You were an answer to this prayer as you sought to lead others to Christ. But so much more remains to be done. No doubt you have discovered more needs than you are capable of meeting. You know firsthand the size of the task of reaching your community for Christ.

To reach our world, more believers must be willing to share Jesus. We must ask God to increase the number of people who share. God gave all Christians the assignment of reaching this world, and it will take all of us to do it.

Jesus called for His followers to "keep asking and it will be given to you" (Matt. 7:7). We pray for almost anything; yet we sometimes forget to pray for the most important things. The challenge of Jesus' words is to keep asking. Praying for more harvest workers must be a regular part of our prayer lives. As long as there is a need for more witnesses to share, there is a need for more prayer.

Take time to ask God to send more people who will share the gospel with others in your community. Ask Him to help you remain a faithful witness for Him.

1. LifeWay research report, 10 March 2006.

FAITH EVANGELISM STORIES

JOE HAD TO DIE

"Joe had to die before I would do what I knew I should do." When David spoke these words, I knew I would never forget them.

Joe was a respected and committed deacon in the church. As a team leader, he had taken David under his wing on his Sunday School class's FAITH team.

But David was discouraged. He felt he had done poorly on their last visit and had not been received well. As a result, he had decided to drop out of FAITH.

"I quit, Joe!"

But Joe's reply was equally startling. "No, David, don't quit now; you'll break up our team. Besides, that family needs something, and I really believe we should return to their home next week and try again!"

David almost swallowed his tongue when he heard Joe's response but managed to say, "Joe, I double quit, because I would never go back into that home!"

David was serious, and as they parted in the parking lot, he told Joe he hoped his dropping off the team would not hinder their friendship.

The next week something bizarre happened. With no forewarning or apparent reason, Joe died suddenly! Everyone in his Oklahoma church was shocked but none like David.

David described his inner struggle: "Now the Holy Spirit was reminding me of Joe's concern to revisit the home where I felt I had bombed out. Plus, I could still hear Joe urging me not to quit and help him make that visit. And now Joe was gone, and I remained!"

David pulled a team together and returned to that home. A wonderful husband and wife were saved that night, along with their two teenage children. They all became members of Joe and David's church and joined a FAITH team themselves. As David stood there with his arms around that couple, he said those unforgettable words: "And just think—Joe had to die before I would do what I knew I should do!"

HELP, I'M DROWNING!

When Jerry stood to speak to us, he did not have the platform presence of an experienced minister of music; he actually looked frail—and for very good reasons!

"After 26 years of marriage, my wife said she did not want to be married any longer. This was made even worse by the fact that I was no longer able to be on the church staff. But as bad as it was, it was about to get worse!

"The doctor discovered a cancerous-looking growth on my brain that had to be removed at M. D. Anderson Hospital. Almost immediately afterward there was another serious surgery to my abdomen, which caused other complications affecting my vision.

"No wife, no children, no job, no church, few if any friends, sick, failing health, and scared, I lay down on the floor of the small, rented upstairs garage apartment just sobbing my heart out: 'Lord, what is happening? Where am I headed? What does all this mean? Why is this happening to me? Where are You, Lord?'

"Just then I heard a knock at my door, and without thinking how I might appear, I opened the door to discover a lady and two men I had never seen. (I discovered later this was a FAITH team from a Sunday School class of a local Baptist church.)

Those people and that visit saved my life that night because I felt as if I were literally drowning in grief, loneliness, sickness, and sorrow, with no one to care.

"They witnessed to me, but I did not need to be saved—I was already saved—but I was drowning. Those three knew how to turn a would-be soul-winning visit into a ministry visit that literally rescued this drowning Christian and changed my life. They picked me up, took me in, cared for me—yes, rescued me!

"I was on their FAITH team last semester but want to lead my own team next semester because I'm just certain there are so many others out there who feel like they are drowning and no one is coming to help. Well, I'm going to try!"

As Jerry concluded with a song, I thought, *Not everyone who is drowning needs to be "saved"; sometimes it is the rescued who need rescuing.*

THE PRODIGAL FATHER

Larry's story of his father illustrates how God can reach even prodigals who have wandered far from home.

It was 1953. My father was an alcoholic drifter running from the police, having robbed grocery and liquor stores while between jobs. My mother, already with three children, was pregnant and becoming increasingly fearful for our safety and sanity. She finally decided to stop all the abuse and madness. My dad was wanted in several northern states, so when Mother told the police about his latest escapades, they immediately arrested him; that was the last time any of us saw him.

We moved to New York when I was three, and we lived there for 17 years, mostly in a government housing project. Welfare and food stamps were all we had while Mother worked hard at odd jobs. One day some people from a Bible-believing church knocked on our door, and my mother accepted Christ. Nine years later I also received Christ, thanks to that same team of visitors.

Life went on, and good things happened for me. I had a family, was the president of my own business, and became a member of a Baptist church. Although my father had never once contacted any of us over the past 44 years, I was overwhelmed with curiosity about him. My wife and I had been intensely searching for more than a year, and I was ready to give up. However, a Social Security worker said we might be able to get a letter to him.

While on a business trip to California, I attempted to write the letter. Later on this trip I called my wife, and she immediately said, "Larry, what would you do if your father came to our door?" Before I could say much, she replied, "Larry, he's here; your father is here!" Remember, I had not even mailed the letter yet.

Arriving home, I met my father, a tiny, emaciated skeleton of a man who looked much older than his age of 80. We spent the next 10 days together. I shared my faith and bought him a Bible that had the plan of salvation in it, but he never received Christ.

Dad went back out west, and our lives went their separate ways. I had just finished my first semester of FAITH training, and I felt confident now that I could present the gospel in an understandable way. Dad had a Bible and a copy of the plan of salvation, but my wife and I now believed he needed to hear about God's saving grace from the heart and lips of someone who loved and cared for him.

We left the East Coast and arrived at the motel room out west, where he lived. After driving around and talking a bit, I asked him the Key Question: "In your personal opinion, what do you understand it takes for a person to get to heaven and have eternal life?" He gave a very unclear works answer and lamented living such a bad life, declaring he would never be welcomed into heaven. I presented the

FAITH outline, and after some clarification he willingly prayed with me to receive Jesus as Savior and Lord.

After 44 years the Lord used FAITH as His way to equip, train, enable, and motivate me to lead my prodigal father to a home in heaven!

JUST IN THE NICK OF TIME

Do you believe in divine appointments? Consider this account from a sister church in Florida.

Our FAITH team from First Baptist Church in Crystal River, Florida, set out to make three visits for our church. The card from the FAITH office was labeled "Please visit this one first." We were ecstatic because the card said the man was interested in finding out how to be a Christian. It was the first visit of the semester, and I had new people on my team. I was anxious about how I would model an actual FAITH visit before them.

Our excitement waned when we went to the home and his neighbor said he was not at home. The neighbor said he might be home around 8:00 p.m. We have our Celebration Time at church at 8:00, so we decided to come back after other visits if we had time.

Our next two visits were in opposite directions. It was now close to 8:00, and we had to decide whether to go to the church or go back to Tom's home. All agreed to go back by his house because we sensed that God was at work.

We arrived at Tom's home, and he greeted us with enthusiasm. He invited us into an apartment with no furniture. We stood in the small kitchen—four adults and a rather large dog that was very friendly. We introduced ourselves, talked about common interests, and asked Tom about his church background. Then Sandy gave her Sunday School testimony. Tom said he had recently moved to our community and had no family here. He had not been in Sunday School since he was a kid. He had come to our church the previous Sunday morning and left a visitor's card stating that he wanted to know how to become a member of our church and how to receive Christ.

It was time for me to ask him the Key Question: "In your personal opinion, what do you understand it takes for a person to get to heaven and have eternal life?" He gave me a works answer, and I was then able to share the gospel. He then prayed a prayer to receive Christ. The tears were flowing. We went through *A Step of Faith* leaflet, kneeling on the bare floor in this empty apartment with the very large dog all over us, probably wondering what we were doing. We enrolled Tom in Sunday School and looked forward to meeting him in church and Sunday School. After completing the leaflet, with all of us signing it and leaving our phone numbers, we left him the baptism information. We were excited about mentoring Tom in his new walk with Jesus. God had answered my prayer to model a FAITH visit from beginning to end for my new trainees.

Pretty typical visit? Now for the rest of the story! The next day our FAITH team went about finding some furniture for Tom. He was working but had been on the job for only a couple of weeks. Our Sunday School class helped, and they had not even met him yet. Tom was so appreciative and surprised that we were helping him, because he had asked us for nothing.

Tom had no transportation, so we were going by to pick him up on Sunday. He didn't answer the door. Later I called his cell phone, and it had been disconnected. We were disappointed because we knew Tom was very sincere when he asked Jesus to come into his life. A couple of days later Tom's neighbor called to tell me that Tom had suffered a massive heart attack on Friday—four days after we had visited him. She had found our numbers on the FAITH material we had left with Tom. We went to the hospital and found him on life support and in a coma.

We became Tom's family, and the church began to pray for him. Our pastor and our team began a vigil of visitation. Tom would move his eyes to indicate that he knew we were there and would turn his head toward us. A week later the doctors took him off life support, and for a while he was even more responsive to our talking. It was hard to leave him after each visit.

On Friday Tom died. But he was not alone. He had a new family of friends, and the best news is that he had a Savior who ushered him into God's presence. He didn't have a long walk with the Lord on this earth, but he is walking with Jesus for eternity. We know that because we were there when Tom said, "Father, I am a sinner. Thank You for forgiving me of my sins, and thank You for saving my soul."

SHARING THE GLAD TIDINGS

The following account is by Jay Johnston, the director of FAITH/Evangelism and Discipleship at LifeWay Christian Resources.

While helping a friend jump-start his car in my driveway, I noticed that I had a nail in my front left tire. My first thought was, *Wow! God, You are so good to let me find that nail in the tire before it goes flat!*

The next day I took the tire to the local Super Wal-Mart where I usually have my car serviced. While I was waiting for them to repair the tire, I walked over to the grocery section of the store. It's a new store, and I had recently asked the store to carry two food items that our family uses. I found that they still did not have the products on the shelves, so I looked for an employee to make another request.

I found a man who was singing and seems to enjoy his work in the fresh-produce section very much. I walked up to him and said, "Hey, I like your singing!"

He smiled and said, "Thanks."

I then asked him about the two items I was looking for in the store. He said the people responsible for those departments were not in the store at the time, but if I wrote down the information, he would be glad to give it to them.

I did so, thanked him, and said, "I have another question for you."

Before I could say anything else, he looked into my eyes and said, "I'm saved."

I smiled and responded, "Tell me about your relationship with Jesus."

He told me his story and then looked at me again and asked, "Are you an angel?"

I assured him that I wasn't but that I was commissioned by Jesus to go through the day sharing His good news. He seemed pleased, and then I called him by name and said, "You know, you can do the same."

He shared the story of how difficult it was to live the Christian life around people at his other job. I encouraged him that, with a smile like his and a story like his, we just needed to pray that God would give him the strength to share the good news. I then went on to say, "You know, you have a great opportunity to share Jesus right here, because the world comes to Wal-Mart!"

He responded with a big smile and said, "I can do that, can't I?"

I smiled back and simply said, "Yes."

We shook hands, and as I started to walk away, he asked, "Are you sure you're not an angel?"

From *SBC LIFE*, April 2002, August 2002, December 2002, September 2004, and December 2005, as reprinted in *Testimonies of Giving Your FAITH Away*, published by the Southern Baptist Convention Executive Committee. Used by permission. All rights reserved.

FAITH EVANGELISM GLOSSARY

Semester: A 12-week time period when FAITH Evangelism training takes place.

FAITH Visits: The FAITH teams conduct five different and distinct types of visits: evangelism visits, ministry visits, Opinion Poll visits, baptism visits, and follow-up visits.

Training sessions: Time periods when FAITH teams meet to learn how to share the FAITH gospel presentation and make FAITH visits. These sessions include Team Time, Teaching Time, Visitation Time, and Celebration Time.

FAITH team: FAITH teams consist of one team leader who has been trained in FAITH Evangelism and two learners who are to be mentored by the trained leader. Ideally, the team represents the same open Bible study group and consists of both male and female members for greater accountability and receptivity when visiting.

Disciple making: A partnership with God, the congregation, and individuals helping people become fully devoted followers of Jesus Christ who are loving, kind, peaceful, good, gentle, faithful, controlled, patient, and joyful.

Facilitator: A person who assists and encourages people to learn. The FAITH Evangelism facilitator leads the training sessions and serves as a FAITH team leader.

Opinion Poll: A survey used by FAITH teams to establish relationships and gather information from people who are not connected to a church.

Team Time: A 15-minute segment of each FAITH Evangelism training session that deals specifically with the gospel presentation and journal work. The team leader guides this dialog.

Teaching Time: A 45-minute segment of each FAITH Evangelism training session that is led by the FAITH facilitator(s).

Visitation Time: A 60- to 90-minute segment of each FAITH Evangelism training session when FAITH teams leave the training location to make visits.

Celebration Time: A 30-minute or less segment of each FAITH Evangelism training session for all of the FAITH teams to come together to evaluate and celebrate their experiences in sharing the gospel.

FAITH learner: Someone who is acquiring knowledge and skill in sharing the gospel and ministering to unchurched persons.

THE ADVENTURE CONTINUES

FAITH EVANGELISM 2 EQUIPS TEAM LEADERS TO MULTIPLY THEIR WITNESS

The life of a Great Commission witness is an ongoing adventure. Those who have been trained to share their faith in *FAITH Evangelism 1* are now ready to become FAITH team leaders and to multiply their witness even further.

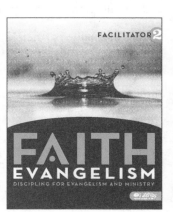

FAITH Evangelism 2 equips FAITH team leaders for their task by teaching them the following skills.
• Influencing team members through spiritual leadership
• Establishing trust and building relationships within the team
• Functioning successfully as a FAITH team
• Overcoming obstacles to effective leadership
• Growing spiritually and helping team members grow
• Mentoring others and encouraging accountability
• Using strengths and spiritual gifts to serve and make disciples
• Connecting disciples to the church
• Staying dependent on God

Make sure your church's FAITH trainees move on to the next great adventure. Use *FAITH Evangelism 2* to build strong spiritual leaders who know how to make an impact for eternity.

Available in June 2008
• *FAITH Evangelism 2 Journal,* item 005035789
• *FAITH Evangelism 2 Facilitator Guide,* item 005035792

TO ORDER, write to LifeWay Church Resources Customer Service; One LifeWay Plaza; Nashville, TN 37234-0113; fax order to (615) 251-5933; e-mail orderentry@lifeway.com; phone toll free (800) 458-2772; order online at www.lifeway.com; or visit the LifeWay Christian Store serving you.

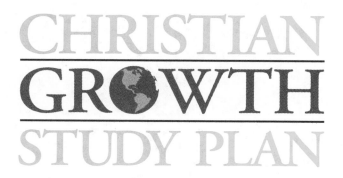

CHRISTIAN GROWTH STUDY PLAN

In the Christian Growth Study Plan, *FAITH Evangelism 1 Journal* is a resource for course credit in the subject areas Evangelism and Discipleship in the Christian Growth category of plans. To receive credit, read the book; complete the learning activities; attend group sessions; show your work to your pastor, a staff member, or a church leader; then complete this form. Send the completed form to:

Christian Growth Study Plan
One LifeWay Plaza; Nashville, TN 37234-0117
Fax (615) 251-5067; e-mail *cgspnet@lifeway.com*

For information about the Christian Growth Study Plan, refer to the *Christian Growth Study Plan Catalog,* located online at *www.lifeway.com/cgsp.* If you do not have access to the Internet, contact the Christian Growth Study Plan office, (800) 968-5519, for the specific plan you need.

FAITH EVANGELISM 1 JOURNAL
CG-1314

PARTICIPANT INFORMATION

Social Security Number (USA ONLY-optional) — — | Personal CGSP Number* — — | Date of Birth (MONTH, DAY, YEAR) — —

Name (First, Middle, Last) | Home Phone —

Address (Street, Route, or P.O. Box) | City, State, or Province | Zip/Postal Code

Email Address for CGSP use

Please check appropriate box: ☐ Resource purchased by church ☐ Resource purchased by self ☐ Other

CHURCH INFORMATION

Church Name

Address (Street, Route, or P.O. Box) | City, State, or Province | Zip/Postal Code

CHANGE REQUEST ONLY

☐ Former Name

☐ Former Address | City, State, or Province | Zip/Postal Code

☐ Former Church | City, State, or Province | Zip/Postal Code

Signature of Pastor, Conference Leader, or Other Church Leader | Date

*New participants are requested but not required to give SS# and date of birth. Existing participants, please give CGSP# when using SS# for the first time. Thereafter, only one ID# is required. **Mail to:** Christian Growth Study Plan, One LifeWay Plaza, Nashville, TN 37234-0117. Fax: (615)251-5067.

Revised 4-05